Give Your Family

A Gift That Money Can't Buy

Record & Preserve Your Family's History

Jeffrey A. Bockman

Family Roots Publishing Co.

www.familyrootspublishing.com

&

Alenjes

www.alenjes.com

Give A Gift That Money Can't Buy
Limited First Edition – 1996

Second Edition booklet – 2005

Third Edition booklet – Minor Revision – 2006

Fourth Edition – Major Revision – 2007

 Library of Congress Control Number: 2007928065
ISBN 978-0-9796173-0-0
Published by Alenjes Publishing, Naperville, IL 60540, www.Alenjes.com

Fifth Edition – Major Revision – 2013

Published by

Family Roots Publishing Company
Bountiful, Utah 84011
www.familyrootspublishing.com

Library of Congress Control Number: 2012954733

ISBN-13: 978-1-933194-88-2
ISBN-10: 1-933194-88-X

All versions printed in the United States of America

Cover Photographs:
- Granville Johnson & Sarah Ellis in 1880, the author's Great Grandparents
- 1357 E. 53rd Street, Chicago, Illinois before 1948, the author's parent's first home
- Miletus Ellis & Mary (Coleman), 1860 to 1870, the author's Great Great Grandparents .
- (Back Cover) Helen Esther DeMary Stevenson, the author's Great Grandmother. Taken between 1875 - 1885 in Chicago, Illinois by Brand.

"A Gift That Money Can't Buy"

Table of Contents

About the Author

Jeffrey A. Bockman, MBA, Genealogy Lecturer and Writer. He has been doing family history and genealogical research since 1988. He has been active in genealogy society management and conference management since 1994.

Speaking engagements have included the 2010 and 2008 Ohio Genealogical Society, the 2006 National Genealogical Society, the 1998, 2001 and 2003 Federation of Genealogical Societies, and the 2000 and 2006 Polish Genealogical Society of America conferences, as well as the 2007 BYU Family History & Genealogy Conference and many other national and regional events.

He was a contributing editor for the former *Everton's Genealogical Helper* and a feature writer for the former *Heritage Quest Magazine*. His articles have also appeared in various publications such as *The Digital Genealogist*, the *FGS Forum*, *Family Tree Magazine (UK)*, *Missing Links*, the *DCGS Review*, and other society publications.

He was the Chairman of the Chicagoland Genealogical Consortium, four term Vice President of the Illinois State Genealogical Society and the President of the DuPage Co. (IL) Genealogical Society for five terms. He was the DuPage County ILGenWeb project webmaster from 1996 to 2012.

Visit www.JeffBockman.com for a list of his upcoming programs,
- **Genealogy and Travel Links** - a list of useful research websites by topic
- **Genealogy According to Jeff** - a wide variety of his articles
- and to: Download forms, View travel photographs, and See more about family history.

Acknowledgments

I would like to thank my parents and all of my ancestors for without them I would not exist and I would not have their stories to share. I am grateful to those that saved and handed down family bible pages, documents, photographs, and their genealogical research. Even those that left almost no clues provided me with the opportunity to improve my research skills. Thanks to my close and distant cousins with whom I have shared friendships, stories, records, emails, and ancestors.

I should also thank one of my twin son's 6th grade teachers who gave a homework assignment to list four great-grandparents. It only took me 22 years to complete that assignment.

After years of collecting ancestors, I attended a series of genealogy classes taught in part by Paul Milner. Thanks to him and a number of other genealogical lecturers I learned the difference between collecting names and dates and doing real research. Thanks also to the DuPage County (IL) Genealogy Society for giving me the opportunity to learn on the job and proving the old adage that the best way to learn something is to teach it. Thanks also to the numerous vendors, libraries, and customers who have supported the earlier editions of this book.

A special thanks goes out to Leland Meitzler for giving me the opportunity to share my knowledge and family stories over the years in *Heritage Quest Magazine* and the *Everton's Genealogical Helper*. He insisted that the forth edition of this book needed a real cover. His Family Roots Publishing Co. LLC is the publisher of record for this edition.

Introduction

The "Give Your Family A Gift That Money Can't Buy" program is intended to encourage and help families preserve their heritage. Use this book as a guide to record, assemble and preserve your memories and family history. Younger family members can use it to learn about their family and hopefully assist their parents and grandparents to create a family heirloom.

When someone becomes interested in learning about the history of their family the first thing they are told to do is to contact older family members and record what they know about their parents, grandparents, and family traditions. Too often people do not become interested until after they have lost a parent and find themselves in a position of being one of the "older" family members.

Children, grandchildren, nieces, and nephews may not be all that interested in the stories right now, but someday they will be interested. Too often that someday is too late. While I spent a lot of time with both of my grandmothers when I was young and I remember a lot of interesting stories, there are a number of questions that I would like to be able to ask them now, especially about their husbands since one died young and the other just left the family.

I was fortunate that many of my ancestors had had photographs taken and that someone had taken the time to write the person's name and occasionally the relationship or the date on the back. Some of the photographs were identified by later generations. A photograph of a person takes them from being just a name and a bunch of dates and helps turn them into a real person.

Reading their letters, diaries, documents, school papers, and stories really helps to show me what they were like, or at least what they were interested in.

➢ Why should you wait for the "young whippersnappers" to come and ask you?

➢ Why depend upon some future relative, or in-law, to dig up information about you and your family from governmental and other records?

➢ Why not sit down and record the information, organize and preserve the documents and photographs that are available, and then tell the stories that only you can tell?

Give your family and descendants **"A Gift That Money Can't Buy."**

The information about your family that should be recorded and preserved is not only for your children but also for their children, and their children.

Even if you did not have any children your nieces and nephews will appreciate the information. You might have knowledge of or a different viewpoint of an event than that of their parents.

Once everything has been assembled, copies can be easily made and shared with all of the other family members.

The time to start is now! Too many people say they will get around to doing it, but unfortunately they never have the opportunity.

The Human Memory

The human memory is a funny thing. While someone may want to fill out everything on a form in order, some of the names, places, or dates just cannot be remembered.

Fill in what is known using a pencil so that changes can be easily made, and then go on to the next section.

Once someone's mind starts hunting around for information it usually comes up with some of the answers. It might be in the middle of the night. Everyone has experienced the "it is on the tip of my tongue" syndrome and then after a while they "remembered" the name of a person or place.

After starting to recall and then talking about events from a particular time period the other associated details will soon come to mind. Your mind stores information by using associations.

While you might not remember someone's birth date you may recall that their birthday party was usually held outside and there was often a football game played on a yard covered with leaves and that one year it snowed all day. You just narrowed it down to the late fall.

Be patient, your mind has to figure out where it stored all of that information and then begin to sift through it since it is no longer stored in the brain's index.

Comments about this Edition

For a number of years I have been giving lectures on the "Give A Gift That Money Can't Buy" program tying to encourage people to record and preserve their family's history. In the lectures I use a number of examples from my family's history. In the 4th edition I included many of those family stories that I hoped were both entertaining and hopefully gave the reader ideas for their own stories.

In this edition I added a few more family stories and photographs.

Once people realize how little they know about their family or when they see a number of blanks in the various forms they often become curious and want to find out how they can fill in some of missing information. For those people and for those that already have an interest in starting to do family history, or genealogical research I have expanded the Family History Research section.

It has been updated to include newer sources, more online resources, a new section on searching techniques, and comments about genealogy travel with examples. There is also a mini case study to hopefully give some hope to those who have a relative that disappeared.

Now is the time to get started.

Start with yourself - Work From Known to Unknown!

Even if you have been given a family tree you need to verify some of it by starting with yourself using Family Facts.

Family Facts

"You cannot tell the players without a scorecard." The first thing that anyone does at a sporting event, ballet, play, opera, or school recital is to look at the program to see who is playing what position, role, or part.

Family relationships can be even more confusing especially when terms have changed over the years. There have been many family histories written that are difficult to follow. Some families have the same names repeated generation after generation and a narrative description of parents and children can get confusing. Before you start using names in stories or on the back of photographs it will be helpful to fill out a scorecard for your family.

Family information can be easily recorded on two basic genealogy forms:

Family Group Sheet   Shows the father and mother along with all of their children. It includes some basic information on each family member.

Ancestor Chart   Shows the father and mother of an individual along with their grandparents, great grandparents and great-great-grandparents. It includes their names along with the dates and the places of their birth, marriage and death. There is also room for basic information on the person's spouse.

Basic rules that apply to both forms:

Filling Out   Use pencil for the first draft so that corrections can be easily made.
Fill in what you can easily remember and then come back later to fill in the missing data as you recall it or find the answers in supporting documents.

Dates: Use the date format **12 Jan. 1875** to prevent any confusion.
The date 8/4/73 is read as
       August 4, 1973 by Americans and as
       April 8 by Europeans
If you do not have an exact date then use the following abbreviations:
Abt = About, Bef = Before, Aft = After, Bet = Between

Names: Use the maiden (birth) name for all females. Show the various husbands and dates on the family group sheet so that the correct name can be determined at any point in time. Document and date any name changes.

Locations: State: Use the standardized Post Office State Abbreviations or spell it out.
Include the county name if it is known: i.e.: Chicago (Cook), IL
Write out the name of any foreign country.

Remember that county and country names may have changed with time. For instance, my grandmother Katherine Kaps was born in the town of Prelesje in Austria, which then became part of Yugoslavia, and it is now in Slovenia.

Family Group Sheet

A Family Group Sheet (FGS) is used to document biological parents and their children. Use a separate Family Group Sheet for each family group: Father, Mother, and Children. Fill in as much information as possible.

Father

♦ Enter the Father's Full Name at the top

♦ Record the date and location of his Birth, Christening, Marriage, Death, and Burial.

♦ Other spouses:
  ➢ Number them with (1), (2), etc. and show each marriage date
  ➢ Create a separate FGS for each partner with which they had children

♦ Fill in his Father's name and his Mother's maiden name. Fill out a FGS for them as well.

♦ The following additional information can be very helpful to find other records:
  ➢ Places of Residence: dates and locations, using additional pages as necessary
  ➢ Occupation: can help to determine the correct person in the census or a city directory
  ➢ Church Affiliation: include the denomination and the specific churches
  ➢ Military Record: list the branch of service, rank, dates, and where stationed

Mother

♦ Enter the Mother's Full Maiden Name (the name she was given at birth)

♦ Complete the same information for her as for the father.

Children

♦ List all of their children, ideally in birth order, and provide the following information:
  ➢ Sex: F-female or M-male
  ➢ Birth date and place
  ➢ If married their Spouse's name, Marriage date and place
  ➢ Death date and place
  ➢ Burial date and place
  ➢ Additional information can be provided such as where they lived or worked
  ➢ Create a separate family group sheet for each child who had children

Compiler

♦ Fill out the compiler's name, address and date information on the bottom

♦ Use the Notes section to continue any entries

Sources

♦ Describe where the information came from, such as a Birth Certificate, Marriage Certificate, or a newspaper article

Family Group Sheet

Father's Full Name

Chart No.

	Day Month Year	City, Town or Place	County or Province, etc.	State or Country	Add. Info. on Husband
Birth					
Chr'nd					
Marr.					
Death					
Burial					

Places of Residence

Occupation | Church Affiliation | Military Rec.

Other wives, if any. No. (1) (2) etc.
Make separate sheet for each marr.

His Father | Mother's Maiden Name

Mother's Full Maiden Name

	Day Month Year	City, Town or Place	County or Province, etc.	State or Country	Add. Info. on Wife
Birth					
Chr'nd					
Death					
Burial					

Places of Residence

Occupation | Church Affiliation | Military Rec.

Other husbands, if any. No. (1) (2) etc.
Make separate sheet for each marr.

Her Father | Mother's Maiden Name

Sex	Children's Names in Full (Arranged in order of birth)	Children's Data		Day Month Year	City, Town or Place	County or Province, etc.	State or Country	Add. Info. on Children
	1		Birth					
			Marr.					
	Full Name of Spouse		Death					
			Burial					
	2		Birth					
			Marr.					
	Full Name of Spouse		Death					
			Burial					
	3		Birth					
			Marr.					
	Full Name of Spouse		Death					
			Burial					
	4		Birth					
			Marr.					
	Full Name of Spouse		Death					
			Burial					
	5		Birth					
			Marr.					
	Full Name of Spouse		Death					
			Burial					
	6		Birth					
			Marr.					
	Full Name of Spouse		Death					
			Burial					
	7		Birth					
			Marr.					
	Full Name of Spouse		Death					
			Burial					
	8		Birth					
			Marr.					
	Full Name of Spouse		Death					
			Burial					

Compiler | Notes:

Address

City, State, Zip

"A Gift That Money Can't Buy"

Ancestor Chart

The Ancestor Chart (also known as a Pedigree Chart) is used to show a person, their parents, their grandparents, etc. for up to five generations. The basic layout is shown below. The chart shows the father and mother for each person along with some basic information on each person.

The information for the Ancestor Chart can be taken directly from the Family Group Sheets.

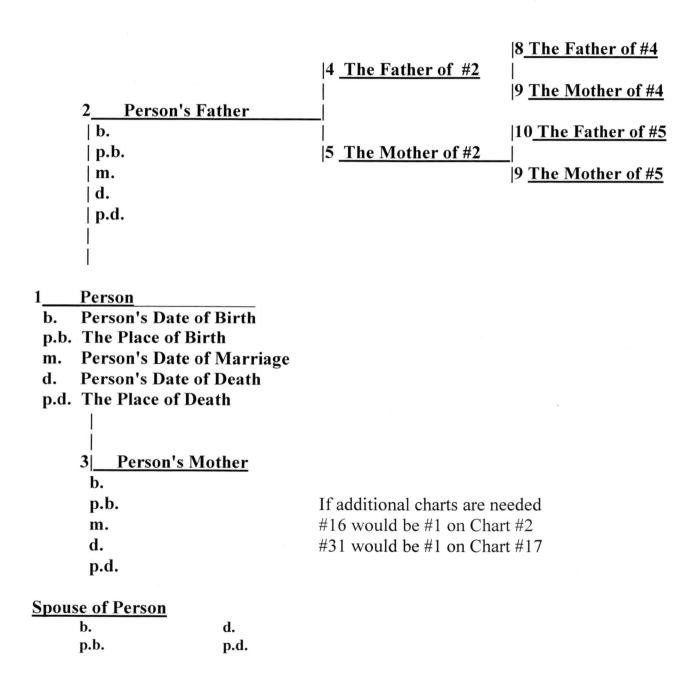

|8 __The Father of #4__

|4 __The Father of #2__

|9 __The Mother of #4__

2___Person's Father_____|

| b. |10 __The Father of #5__

| p.b. |5 __The Mother of #2___|

| m. |9 __The Mother of #5__

| d.

| p.d.

1___Person_____

  b.   **Person's Date of Birth**
  p.b. **The Place of Birth**
  m.   **Person's Date of Marriage**
  d.   **Person's Date of Death**
  p.d. **The Place of Death**

3|___Person's Mother__

  b.
  p.b.
  m.
  d.
  p.d.

If additional charts are needed
#16 would be #1 on Chart #2
#31 would be #1 on Chart #17

__Spouse of Person__

  b.   d.
  p.b.   p.d.

Ancestor Chart

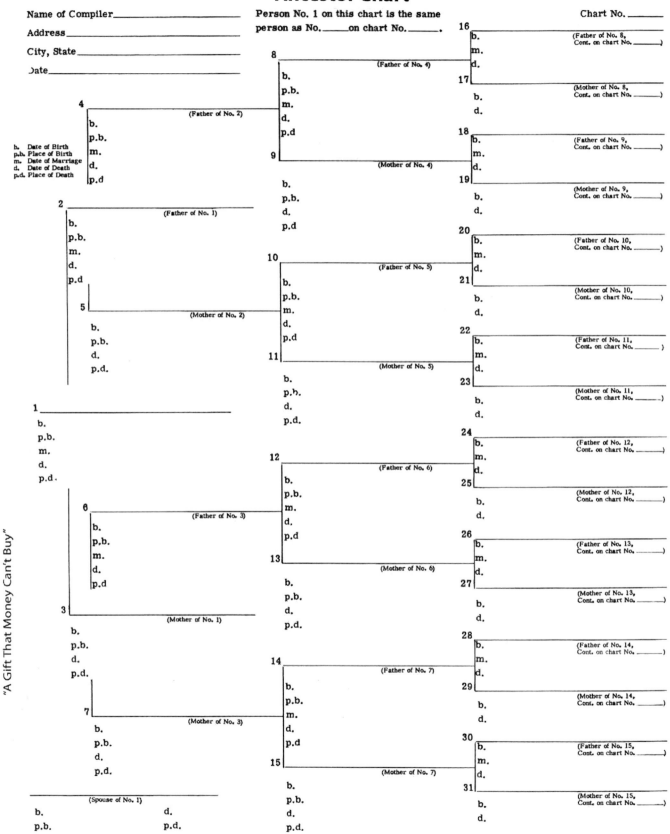

Name of Compiler_____

Address_____

City, State_____

Date_____

Person No. 1 on this chart is the same person as No._____ on chart No._____.

Chart No._____

b. Date of Birth
p.b. Place of Birth
m. Date of Marriage
d. Date of Death
p.d. Place of Death

8 (Father of No. 4)
b.
p.b.
m.
d.
p.d

9 (Mother of No. 4)
b.
p.b.
d.
p.d

4 (Father of No. 2)
b.
p.b.
m.
d.
p.d

2 (Father of No. 1)
b.
p.b.
m.
d.
p.d

5 (Mother of No. 2)
b.
p.b.
d.
p.d.

1 _____
b.
p.b.
m.
d.
p.d.

10 (Father of No. 5)
b.
p.b.
m.
d.
p.d

11 (Mother of No. 5)
b.
p.b.
d.
p.d.

6 (Father of No. 3)
b.
p.b.
m.
d.
p.d

3 (Mother of No. 1)
b.
p.b.
d.
p.d.

7 (Mother of No. 3)
b.
p.b.
d.
p.d.

12 (Father of No. 6)
b.
p.b.
m.
d.
p.d

13 (Mother of No. 6)
b.
p.b.
d.
p.d.

14 (Father of No. 7)
b.
p.b.
m.
d.
p.d

15 (Mother of No. 7)
b.
p.b.
d.
p.d.

(Spouse of No. 1)
b.   d.
p.b.   p.d.

16 b.
m.
d. (Father of No. 8, Cont. on chart No._____)

17 b.
d. (Mother of No. 8, Cont. on chart No._____)

18 b.
m.
d. (Father of No. 9, Cont. on chart No._____)

19 b.
d. (Mother of No. 9, Cont. on chart No._____)

20 b.
m.
d. (Father of No. 10, Cont. on chart No._____)

21 b.
d. (Mother of No. 10, Cont. on chart No._____)

22 b.
m.
d. (Father of No. 11, Cont. on chart No._____)

23 b.
d. (Mother of No. 11, Cont. on chart No._____)

24 b.
m.
d. (Father of No. 12, Cont. on chart No._____)

25 b.
d. (Mother of No. 12, Cont. on chart No._____)

26 b.
m.
d. (Father of No. 13, Cont. on chart No._____)

27 b.
d. (Mother of No. 13, Cont. on chart No._____)

28 b.
m.
d. (Father of No. 14, Cont. on chart No._____)

29 b.
d. (Mother of No. 14, Cont. on chart No._____)

30 b.
m.
d. (Father of No. 15, Cont. on chart No._____)

31 b.
d. (Mother of No. 15, Cont. on chart No._____)

"A Gift That Money Can't Buy"

9

Home Sources

There are a number of documents that you might have at home that can help to provide the information that you need to fill out the various forms. The three most common records are:

- ➤ Birth Certificate: Baby's name, the date and place of birth, the mother's maiden name, parents' names and ages, and the state or possibly city of their birth
- ➤ Marriage License: Names of the bride and groom, their ages, the date and place of the marriage. On a rare occasion, it may include their parent's names.
- ➤ Death Certificate: Name of the deceased, the date, place, the cause of death, and possibly the cemetery and funeral home. It may also include their birth date and their parents' names.

The Home/Family Sources page contains a list of items that might be found in your home or at the home of your parents or another relative. Some of these items can provide information to help you fill out the forms. Many of them should be saved for future generations. See the Preservation section.

Primary & Secondary Evidence

All of the forms contain a combination of primary & secondary information.

Primary Evidence: Facts about the event that were witnessed and reported at that time.

A birth certificate will show that a baby was born at a location on a specific date. It will also show the name of the mother and possibly who delivered the baby. These facts are all primary evidence.

Secondary Evidence: Information about the people that was not witnessed.

The quality of the information will depend upon the informant, the person who provided the information.

A birth certificate might show the city or state where the mother was born along with her age. This is all secondary evidence since it was not witnessed and was based only upon what was stated by the woman or her spouse.

Similarly, a Death Certificate may also contain information about the deceased's spouse, birth, and parents. This is all secondary evidence and the validity of it will depend a great deal upon the informant. If a man's wife is the informant, and her maiden name is listed, that would make it a primary source. Nobody that was present at the death of a 90 year old person would have first hand knowledge of their birth or the birthplace of their parents.

A friend of mine has her great grandmother's death certificate, where the son-in-law was the informant. The only correct information on the certificate is that which pertains to the death!

Home/Family Sources

Too often when "downsizing" from the old family home into an apartment, condo or retirement community, people throw out valuable documents that a future family historian would treasure. Having the names and dates is good, but it is the home sources that can provide the proof that is needed. They also provide a lot of interesting information, clues, and insights about the people.

Family
Family Bible
Family History
Family Traditions
Oral History

Birth/Parents
Adoption Records
Baby Books
Baptismal Certificates
Birth Announcements
Birth Certificates
Confirmation Certificates

Marriage
Marriage Announcements
Marriage Certificates
Wedding Guest Books
Anniversary Guest Books
Divorce Papers

Death
Cemetery Receipts
Death Announcements
Death Certificates
Funeral Cards
Funeral Home Receipts
Funeral Services
Memorial Cards
Probate Records
Sympathy Cards
Wills

Citizenship
Passports
Emigration Papers
Immigration Papers
Naturalization Papers
Drivers Licenses
Motor Vehicle Registration
Voter Registration

Personal Interest/Clues
Address Books
Autograph Books
Diaries
Family correspondence
Greeting Cards
Invitations
Journals
Letters, Envelopes
Medical Records
Newspaper Clippings
Photo Albums
Post Cards
Programs
Scrapbooks
Social Security Cards
Telegrams

Business/Finance
Account Books
Bank Books
Business Cards
Business License
Check Stubs
Credit Statements
Company Advertisements
Employment Records
Family Business Papers
Insurance Papers
Stock Certificates
Tax Returns/Receipts

Employment
Payroll Slips
Professional Papers
Promotion Letters
Resume
Union Cards

Social
Fraternal Memberships

Land
Land Deeds
Mortgage Papers
Property Survey
Property Tax Records

Military
Draft Cards
Military Awards
Military Discharge Papers
Military Enlistment Papers
Military Service Records

School
School Enrollment
Diplomas
Graduation Records
School - Report Cards
School -Transcripts
School -Year Books

Heirlooms
Photographs - identified
Signed & dated Art work
Furniture
- Take photographs
- Document its history
Wedding Dress

Create
Chronological Lists of:
♦ Addresses where lived
♦ Schools attended
♦ Employers

Chronological Lists / Timelines

A Timeline is a useful tool to be able to see events in chronological order. It is especially good for documenting where people lived, went to school, and worked. A timeline can be created for a single person documenting all of the events in their life or one can be created for a specific topic. See the Bockman vacation timeline in the Family Stories section that shows the year, the type of car, the destination, and some key events. They are also a good way to start outlining the events for writing your family story.

Creating them on a computer spreadsheet or table is easier than using a paper form because you can insert events or sort them by date. If you are using the forms provided, add events at the top, middle or end of the form to get them close to the proper order. You can always rewrite or type them into order at a later date. The most important thing is to get the information recorded.

Addresses

Knowing when and where a person lived will help a future researcher locate records. A location or address can often be used to help identify the correct record when there is more than one person with the same name. Addresses can often be found on the birth certificates of their children, utility and tax bills, letters and on a variety of other records.

Some people keep items like old utility bills, letters, and tax returns. Before discarding these types of records, use them to help create the list since they might show within a year or even the month when they moved from one place to another.

Sample Address Timeline for my mother's family between 1929 and 1938.

Photo #	Years	Address	Location
8,10	1929-30	643 Downer Place by RR - (duck, fire, trolley, train)	Aurora, IL
	1930	Island Homes	Knoxville, TN
	1930	West End Place, by College	Knoxville, TN
	1931	Holstein Hills,	Knoxville, TN
2	End 1931	300 W. Downer Place – lower level in back	Aurora, IL
1	1932	2?? Odd NE Corner Downer & Locust – Apt Bldg	Aurora, IL
	1932-34	255 Downer Place	Aurora, IL
5,7		518 Downer Place	Aurora, IL
6		519 Downer Place	Aurora, IL
12		827 Downer Place	Aurora, IL
9	1941 - 48	647 Downer Place - 2nd floor apartment	Aurora, IL

Photographs of each location could be inserted in an electronic version.

Schools and Employment

Use a timeline or a written format similar to a résumé to show all of the schools attended, including elementary, along with a list of all of the places of employment and the job title. A good researcher like a hiring manager will wonder about any gaps.

Important Home Sources

Family Bible

A family bible where different generations have recorded the births, deaths and marriages of various family members is an invaluable resource, especially for a future researcher. A bible can be used to document events when there are no official records available. If you have the bible, you want to make sure that it is stored safely and that copies or photographs are made of the title page and any pages that contain the family events. Do not add any events that you did not have first hand knowledge of. Adding historic events will cast doubt on the validity of all of the information.

Newspaper Clippings

Birth, marriage and death announcements, stories about the family business, sporting achievements, society news, arrest reports, news stories, and possibly even a photograph. Family members will probably have saved them all except for possibly the arrest reports and thrown them in a drawer or scrapbook. These stories often let you learn much more about the person that just the basic facts.

Diary

A person's diary can give insight into their interests and thoughts. It may tell about their daily activities and who they talked with or visited. It can also contain information about some of the major events in their life or the lives of their family members and close friends.

I knew of one person whose grandmother wrote down all of the details about family births, marriages, and deaths in the margins of her cookbook on whatever page was open at the time.

Calendars with the various appointments and notes written on it can be saved as a sort of diary and are useful to help refresh your memory.

Letters

Not the "A" to "Z" ones, but the old-fashioned method of communication where people actually wrote on pieces of paper and mailed them in an envelope. Besides the information contained in the letter, the envelope has the person's address, the sender's address, and the date that it was postmarked.

I have two 100 year-old letters from different great-grandfathers where one was trying to find out more about his father's family and the other letter was talking about how the kids today don't know about or care that much about the family's history.

Unfortunately, today there will be no record kept of family communications unless some of the more interesting and important e-mails are printed out and saved. Write the person's real name and address or location on the copy since nobody will know who "funtime21@xyz.com" is in the future.

Handling Sensitive Topics

Home sources may be one way to provide details about topics that you may not care to discuss but that should still be recorded for future generations. You can just save the key documents, news articles, and photographs or create a written account of the details. If you prefer, it could then be sealed and saved along with instructions in your will as to who should receive it.

Bockman Family Home Sources

Here are a few examples of how my family handled or didn't handle some sensitive situations.

My grandfather Alvar Bockman left his wife having to care for four small children. My grandmother then destroyed all photographs and any references of him and never spoke of him again.

I spent over twenty years trying to find and learn about his parents. It was difficult since Alvar was reportedly born in Central America to European parents, who were supposedly killed during one of the numerous revolutions in Nicaragua. A photograph of him or the names of his parents would have been invaluable. His older children had a few memories of him but they didn't appear to care that much about him either. Unfortunately, as a result the younger children and all future generations have a large segment of their family history that is missing.

He must have had some good features for someone to marry him and have four children. It would be nice to know what they were. (See "Finding Alvar" on page 48 for an update on my research.)

While growing up I was aware of my father's progressive paralysis. I had seen pictures of him as a healthy ballplayer, dancer, and doing acrobatics when he was younger but we never really discussed the time period, shortly before I was born, when he became ill.

Bockman nicks Holloway for the long safety of the Englewood tilt.

I came across several of his scrapbooks, after I had grown up, that were filled with photographs and newspaper clippings. One of the newspaper clippings told of his illness. The Broadway column by Danton Walker included "The youngsters in the ballet of "Song of Norway" are taking up a collection for one of their former members, Charles Bockman, stricken with a malady which will eventually paralyze him. Any contributions for his medical care will be appreciated."

There was also a get-well card signed by many of the cast members along with *The Playbill*.

This was his way of dealing with that time period.

Reading that article and seeing the card for the first time was very difficult for me because it was the first time that I had ever dealt with the period when he first became ill. It was also hard knowing that even with all of the cast's get-well wishes it would not help.

So what did my father do after being told that he could no longer dance?

He came back home to Chicago and opened up a dancing school.

In looking through his old ledger books I found out that on May 9, 1947 my future mother and three long-term family friends all became his students. All four of them went on to have successful dance careers.

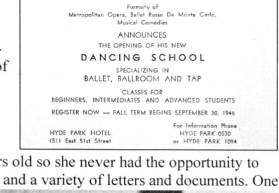

Letters Home

My mother's father died when she was only three years old so she never had the opportunity to know him. Fortunately her mother saved photographs and a variety of letters and documents. One of the items saved and handed down was a box that contained about 90 letters that he had written home to her while he was stationed in France during World War I. There was also a notebook with all of his military orders and official letters.

His early letters said "Somewhere in France" and "Somewhere else in France" because all of the letters were being censored to make sure that they didn't divulge anyone's exact location.

I was able to determine where the letters were written based upon the date of the letter and comparing them to a timeline that I had created by reviewing his military orders and seeing where he was stationed on various dates.

His letters give us a brief glimpse into some of his interests and observations along with what he was doing. He said that he was unable to write any details about the training that he was receiving but that it was very interesting and that he would tell about it when he got back home.

Here is a portion of his April 29, 1918 letter sent while in training at Is Sur Tille, France which is north of Dijon in the Burgundy region.

Grandfather Jack with my Aunt

Yesterday was a lovely day - for a change, & I took a long bicycle ride through out the country - it was lovely - but oh boys! My setter is ruined. This county is very hilly - but perfectly beautiful! Some of the views from hilltops are exquisite - & in the early a.m. the grotesque effects are wonderful - sort of a blue haze - with poplars sticking through dimly. Must go, more later.

5:00 p.m. at the Club

Finished class early today - so beat it up here to finish this letter. The new work is very interesting - our instructor is a French Major & he is a dandy - speaks splendid English & his explanations are very clear & easy to grasp, although the subject is complicated.

Must tell you about our mess - I belong to two - one where we live & one where we work - Breakfast & supper at the first & lunch as the other - saves a long hike up hill. Our meals are usually very good - yesterday we ate up six big turkeys (roast) at noon mess - Breakfast consists of cereal or mush, toast, French fried spuds, wieners or ham - jam & coffee or cocoa. Lunch - Meat usually veal salad, vegetables - fresh radishes, onion lettuce - watercress, mashed boiled or FF spuds - French peas - wheat bread, jam & bully mince pie & coffee. All this is well cooked & it costs in Francs five a day!!! Not quite $1.00!!! You couldn't put any one of the meals for $1.00 - even if you could buy the material under the law. Thank heaven there are no restrictions on food

He included a lot of details about his living accommodations and there was even a sketch of one of his rooms at Is Sur Tille.

There were numerous updates on his increasing weight during the voyage over and the first few months of training. His weight went back down once he started walking several miles a day around the ordinance depots. I have an artillery shell casing that he brought back home. Other letters commented on the news that the family back home was moving to a new house or of the death of a friend or neighbor.

Since my mother was not born until over a year and a half after his return I am very happy that he was safely managing ordinance well away from the front lines. I have found almost every available genealogical record about my grandfather but his letters are the only things that give us any insight into him as a person.

Clues

The various home sources that have been handed down have enabled me to learn a lot more about my ancestors as people and not just as a collection of names and dates. One day my mother asked me if a small newspaper clipping would be helpful. It helped to establish a cousin connection between a Johnston family in Virginia and our family and it provided clues for trying to track down a claimed family bible. Yes, that small newspaper clipping was helpful.

At a crime scene every clue is important and even the tiniest thread or a hair can help to break a case. Home sources are the clues for a family history researcher.

Photographs

"A picture is worth a thousand words."

An identified photograph of a great-great grandparent is worth even more. From the time a child is born everyone is saying something like "the baby has their mother's eyes" or "their father's chin." Here is a chance to see and compare several generations and see who really resembled whom. With pictures you might even be able to see how different generations looked at the same age.

Having the names and dates on a form is a good start; however it provides a very skeletal view of a person. Having a photograph really helps to turn them into a real person. Finding a photograph of people that cannot be identified or are only partially identified, for example, "Aunt Martha in 1912," is extremely frustrating. Seeing photographs where someone took the time to write the names and dates on the back sitting in antique shops is equally frustrating.

Please take the time to identify and preserve your family's photographic treasures.

A Brief History of Photography to help identify the approximate date range

Daguerreotype: Popular from 1839 to 1855. About 3,000,000 were produced. Usually framed under glass in an attractive hinged case that was often covered with velvet. The picture appears as a negative when viewed from an angle.

Ambrotype: Usually produced between 1854 and 1870. Image on a sensitized glass, sometimes ruby colored, with black paper or painted black backing.

Tintypes: Introduced in 1854 and used until 1900. The picture image is on a very thin sheet of black japanned metal.

They were often framed with a decorative copper edging. Some were also mounted under glass and/or put in an attractive hinged case.

The example, at right, shows Miletus & Mary Ellis.

Cabinet Cards	Beginning in 1866, paper based photograph mounted on a 4.5 inch by 6.5 inch heavy cardboard backing. The photographer's name and address were usually printed on the border or on the back. Right: Reduced image of a cabinet card of Beulah Brown.	
Carte-de-Visite	Smaller paper based photographs mounted on a 2.5 inch by 4.5 inch heavy cardboard backing. The photographer's name and address were usually printed on the border or on the back. See Helen DeMary's photo (back cover).	
Kodak	1884: George Eastman developed flexible roll film. 1888: Eastman's roll-film "string camera" introduced. Round 2.75 inch photos, sample on next page. 1930s: Good reasonably priced color film became available. 1970s: Many prints turned orange or were stored in PVC albums.	

Polaroid   1950s Instant photographs produced without negatives. The photos needed to be coated with a preservative. Over time those that were poorly coated have faded or streaked. The quality and durability improved in later years. Copies can only be made from the original.

Modern day   Faster and cheaper film and cameras resulting in more photographs under various conditions; low light, high speed action, etc.

Digital   Early prints did not use archival paper or inks and will fade.
File storage on disk, CDROM, or DVD will need to be constantly converted to the current format to be able to read them.

Slides, Movies, Videotapes, Digital Video
Future generations could have the option of seeing and hearing the birth of their great grandparents in addition to graduations, sporting events, and weddings.
Make sure that you also preserve the mechanical means to display or play them, or transfer them to the current medium before it is obsolete. An interview stored on an old "wire recorder" reel is useless without a wire recorder to play it.

Family Photographs

You might be lucky to have even one photograph of some relatives. This "string camera" photo of Hiram Demary was taken by his daughter Helen Stevenson in 1890. During the 1940s the number of photographs for each person grew as photography became easier and more affordable. Since the 1970s the number of photographs of an individual could easily number into the hundreds. Now, with digital cameras there could be thousands of images for some individuals.

For this project try to select, identify, and preserve the best photos for each person at various stages of their life. People will then be able to identify other pictures using these photos as a guide.

Selecting - Since children change rapidly there should be a concentration of yearly school or other photos. There could also be photos of major events, such as: graduations, weddings, new homes, children, pets, vacations, etc. This is not intended to be the ultimate photo album but a collection to help identify an individual and preserve the best photographs.

There may be some photographs that you cannot identify, so identify as much as you can. Narrow down the choices as much as you can. Even knowing which side of the family they came from can help. Ask other family members since they may be able to recognize the person or the place. Save the pictures! You may be able to identify them in the future with help from another photograph, a book, or some another source.

Identify everyone in a photograph to help future generations or even you in a few years. The following is the type of information that you should write on the back of the print:

Full Name	Include the full maiden and all married names. A photo with "Mary Elizabeth Coleman Ellis Berkey" written on the back let me find her second marriage and information about her death and burial. The back of Beulah Brown's cabinet card had "Beulah Brown daughter of Lucy Lenore Ellis Brown" written on it, providing her mother's maiden name.
Date	Use the 12 Jan 1996 format.
Location	Tell where the photo was taken. "On vacation in Estes Park, Colorado." "Home on 53rd Street" is OK if you have listed all of the addresses in the family history or on a timeline.

Documenting Photographs

- ➤ Do not write on the front (image side) of a photograph
- ➤ Write on the back, while it is on a hard surface, using light pressure
- ➤ Use a soft lead or a #6 pencil if writing on paper backing
- ➤ Use an archival film-marking pen if writing on modern resin backed photos
- ➤ Make sure the archival ink is dry before stacking them
- ➤ Do no cut original photographs. Older photos may lose the image if cut.
- ➤ Make a copy of a picture to display or for use in a scrapbook

Preservation

Preservation is stabilizing the condition of an artifact to minimize or prevent deterioration. Restoration is restoring items that have become damaged and is beyond the scope of this book.

You want to make sure that future generations will be able to enjoy the various forms, documents, photographs, certificates, books, photographs, newspapers, etc. that you have. How you preserve and store these materials will be the way that they are kept for many years to come. If not stored properly, about the time that the value of the material is finally appreciated it could be too late.

The materials being preserved will need:

> **Protection** from mechanical or physical damage, excessive handling, oils and perspiration, acidic fumes, visible and ultraviolet light, insects, rodents and normal decay.

> **Preparation** for storage that makes it more usable, and limits future damage while not causing further damage. Do not do anything that cannot be undone, such as lamination.

> **Storage** in the appropriate type of container and location to: allow the desired access, protect it from hazards, and limit the expose to further damage.

General Storage Recommendations

Many of the common storage products and practices used in most homes actually harm the items more than preserve them. Many family photo albums from the 1970s were made with PVC, polyvinyl chloride, pages that emit hydrochloric acid as they deteriorate and chemically damage the photographs they were supposed to protect. The cardboard boxes and shoeboxes often used to store papers and photographs produce an acid as they chemically degrade. The acid migrates to the less acidic paper that you are trying to preserve. Oak cabinets produce similar acids as do some wood finishes. The following comments apply to most items being stored.

Handling:

> Handle all items gently
> Documents: Wash and thoroughly dry your hands before handling original documents.
> Photographs: Use clean light cotton gloves or handle by the edges to prevent fingerprints or hand oil stains

Sheet & Photo Protectors:

These should be made from:

> Polyester (Mylar):   Used for sheet protectors and encapsulations
> Polyethylene: Used for photographic and document sleeves
> Polypropylene: Used for 35mm slide or film sleeves and containers

These are all odorless. Do not use PVC or anything with a "new car" smell

Containers:

Storage boxes should be "archival" quality. They should be acid-free and lignin free.
There are two primary styles for regular 8.5" x 11" size papers:

➤ Archival Document Case: With a fold over top for easy access where documents are stored upright in acid-free folders. An adjustable spacer should be used to keep the folders upright and prevent sagging if the box is not full. These are also available for legal sized documents.

➤ Flat Storage Box: with a drop side , hinged lid or clamshell design to allow easy access.

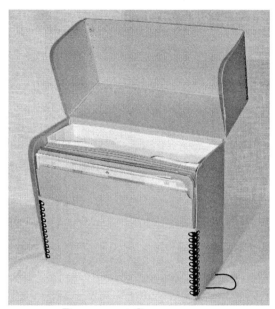
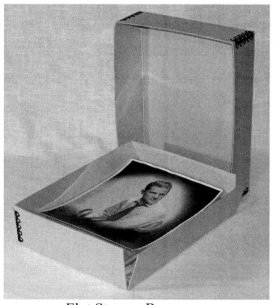

Document Case   Flat Storage Box

Location: Store items in a safe environment

➤ Temperature & Humidity: The ideal conditions are 60° Fahrenheit with 40% Relative Humidity. Extreme temperature changes should be avoided. Avoid storage in a basement, attic or garage. An interior main floor closet is a good alternative.

➤ Light: Sunlight can fade displayed photographs and documents.
Display a copy or use a frame with ultra-violet filter Plexiglas.
Storage boxes can become heated if stored where exposed to direct sunlight

➤ Hazards: Consider all possible situations and take reasonable precautions.
Do not store items directly below an area with potential water damage from a roof or pipe leak or an appliance overflow.
Fireplace sparks and smoke damage from a down draft should also be avoided.

Storing a copy in a different location is good insurance against a fire, tornado or other disaster.
Valuable originals could be stored in a fireproof safe or bank vault.
Electronic images can also be made with the backup copies stored in multiple locations.

Paper & Document Preservation

Important papers and documents are more fragile than you may think. They need to be handled and stored carefully to ensure their long-term survival. Many of these items were not made from the highest quality materials. The high acid content of low quality paper products is a big problem. When paper products age they become brittle (will break with one or two folds) and yellow.

While you would like to preserve the original document so that it can be handed down to future generations it is just as important to insure that the information is also available. Copies of the original can be made on archival quality paper. If you want one to display then use the copy to prevent fading from exposure to light. The original and a copy should be stored separately to prevent damage to both items from a flood, fire, water leak, or other catastrophe.

Newsprint is highly acidic and should not be stored with other types of paper. Archival copies should be made of all articles and clippings that you wish to preserve. The original newsprint copies can be stored with buffered tissue to counteract the acids.

Preparation: Carefully remove nonessential items such as paper clips, staples, and rubber bands without causing damage to the material. Do not use a staple remover since it will tear the paper; use a flat tool and bend the ends straight upward and manually pull out. If the paper is not brittle unfold it, let it relax, and then store it flat. If it is very brittle then you will need help from a restoration expert.

Storage: The type of storage depends upon the desired future use:

➤ Papers in good condition that will be handled often should be stored in an archival sheet protector, in an archival quality folder in an upright storage box. If the document needs additional support then it should be stored in polyester sleeve or it should be encapsulated between two polyester sheets using archival quality double-sided tape.

➤ Papers that will not be handled can be stored in a flat storage box using acid-free tissue to prevent contact with other items. All items in the box should be about the same size as the box to prevent items moving around and causing damage.

Photo Preservation

Negatives are actually more important than the photograph since new prints can be created from the negative. See the preservation chapter for the care of them. When selecting photographs to identify and preserve, keep the negative with the photo and preserve both.

Old photographs should be preserved for future generations. If you want to display the photo then a photographic copy should be made and the copy displayed. An extra can also be made and stored separately from the original. This can be done at many photo shops while you wait. A digital camera or scanner can be used to create an electronic image that can be printed at a photo shop. Larger documents can be easily reduced to an 8.5 by 11 inch size for easy use or display.

Modern photographs present a problem in that there is probably such a large volume that it will be impractical to preserve them all. If an important photograph was damaged from or stuck in a PVC "magnetic" album or it has faded then print a new copy from the negative if it is available. Otherwise you should scan or take a digital photo of it and just leave it in the old album rather than possibly destroying it while trying to remove it.

Storage: DO NOT store slides, negatives or prints in the boxes or envelopes used by the film developer. Photographs, slides and negatives should be stored in "acid-free" sleeves specifically designed for them:

- Photo sleeves come in various formats to hold different sizes.
- They allow easy viewing while offering protection and support.
- Photographs that need additional support should be stored in a polyester sleeve.

Photographic Protection Sleeves

Prints can also be stored in archival boxes if kept in areas of low humidity.

If you have an old photo album from an ancestor that you do not want to take apart

- Use pieces of acid-free unbuffered tissue between each page
- Provide protection or support by using an archival storage box or enclosure

Finding Supplies

Archival-quality products can often be purchased at a good photo or office supply store. Museum stores, hobby, and craft stores can also be good sources. See www.hollingermetaledge.com and www.gaylord.com for a wide variety of archival products.

Family Stories

The FGS lists only the marriage and the birth of children between a person's birth and death. Obviously there is much more that can and needs to be told. Take this opportunity to tell about yourself and your family, especially the time period before the next generation was old enough to remember. Also include the stories about your parents, grandparents, and other family members.

Try to write about situations that show what you or someone else was really like. Tell about the things that were really important to you or your family. Tell the stories that make your family "Your Family." Tell those stories that cause your family to laugh at the mention of a single word or place.

Write them down; Type it out; Use a computer. If you do not like to write and cannot type then use audio or video tapes to let future generations hear and/or see you. It **will** be appreciated someday by somebody who really wants to know more about you. Please, DO NOT WAIT.

Tell the stories that only you can tell. To help get you started, start telling about your:

Childhood: Family pets, friends, the neighborhood where you grew up, neighbors, local stores and merchants, after school activities, hobbies, favorite music, chores you did around the house, recreational activities or sports, bedtime stories and religious upbringing.
Favorite memories of your parents, grandparents and other relatives

Schooling: Grammar, High School, College, other
Favorite teachers and classes, best friends
What extracurricular activities did you participate in?

Military Service: Branch of Service, unit, commanders, etc. How and why you joined. Where were you trained or stationed? Describe your experiences. Did you fight in a war? Did you have any special training or learn foreign languages?

Personal: Nickname(s), close friends, favorite food and restaurants, Hobbies, things of importance to you, athletics, activities, etc. Favorite music, books, art, jokes, stories, places to visit. Stories about your pets, friends, famous acquaintances and religious beliefs. Feelings during important events (wars, assassinations, moon landing, etc.). How technology changes have affected you and your life. Places you lived and the dates. Accomplishments.

Occupation: What was your first job? Where did you work and what did you do?

Family: Where did you first see your future spouse? Where did you meet for the first time? Tell about your engagement, marriage, honeymoon, etc. Describe your first apartment, purchasing your first home, and pets.

Children: Tell about the birth of your children, stories about your children growing up: school, sports, favorite foods, funny stories, family vacations, and holidays.

Grandchildren: Stories about your grandchildren growing up, visits, activities together.

Timeline of Events

An easy way to get started telling about your life is to fill out a timeline or create a chronological list of the various major events in your life. You can also complete one for your spouse and each of your parents. Create a table similar to the following or copy one of the forms near the end of this book. You can then choose to write about some of the events in greater detail.

Full Name:		
Date	**Event**	**Comments**
	Birth	

Enter the person's full birth name and then start entering Events beginning with their birth.

Manual entries will probably not be in exact chronological order. It is easier to insert or sort the events into date order if it is done on a computer.

DATE - Dates can be exact (1 Feb. 1945) or a range (June - Aug. 1957).

EVENT - Types of events shown, plus whatever is of interest to you.

Types	**Comments / also Give Full Source Reference**
Adoption	Full names of parents or child
Alias	Give full alias name
Annulment	Give place and details
Arrival	Place, Name of Ship and Captain, Sailed from
Baptism	Place: Church, City, etc, Officials & Witnesses
Camp	Name, Location, Activities
Census	Year, State, County, name in household
Church	Name, Location, Activities
Destination	Place that they were going to
Dwelling	Give Full Address
Education	Name and location of School
Graduation	Name and location of School
Living	Give Full Address, City, County, State, Country
Medical	Illness, Operation, duration, hospital, doctor, etc.
Military	Branch of Service, Where stationed, Duties
Naturalization	State, City and Jurisdiction
Organization	Names, duties, titles, etc.
Occupation	Jobs: Company, duties, title, etc.
Probate	Location, jurisdiction
Title	Description
Vacation	Places visited and type of transportation
Will	Where filed, witnesses / When probated

Write COMPILED BY: and then your name and the date at the bottom.

Bockman Family History - Excerpts

Vacations - While growing up, one of the main things that made our family "our family" were our Summer Vacations. They represented much more than just where we went. They showed some of our interests, explained our somewhat strange sense of humor, and our sense of adventure. These were the shared experiences that were a major part of and influenced our family life.

Every August from 1956 to 1970, except for 1961 when we moved, my mother and father closed the Dance Studio, loaded up the car and we all went on a month long vacation. When we left home we often had little more than a general direction or a few destinations. We never had a reservation. Over the years we went to every continental US State, except for Delaware, Louisiana, Mississippi and Alabama. We also went throughout Mexico, almost to Guatemala and every lower province of Canada from Gaspe, Quebec to Vancouver Island and north to Timmons, Ontario and even Jasper, Alberta before there was a paved road. One year we spent eight hours lost in the middle of Monument Valley, Arizona, again before paved roads, digging the car out of the red sand, with only three cans of RC Cola to drink.

Our adventures included: driving until 2:00 AM looking for a motel room in Wisconsin, coasting down mountain roads in Mexico with the engine turned off to keep from running out of gas (before power steering and brakes), having extended visits in several small towns while our car was being fixed, watching bears eat our food in Yellowstone, and holding the ropes of a roof rack to keep it from sliding over the windshield. Our cars and our vacations were our calendar and many of the other events in our lives were associated with them:

Year	Car	Destinations
1955	47 Pontiac	Yellowstone, Tetons, Mt. Rushmore, Badlands
1956	47 Pontiac	Colorado, Monument Valley, Grand Canyon, Las Vegas, Taos
1957	51 Buick	Western Canada, Glacier Park, Yellowstone
1958	51 Buick	Mexico to Acapulco & Oaxaca - "Betsy Buick" limped home
1959	56 Buick	Colorado, Ouray
1960	56 Buick	California, Yosemite, San Francisco, Coast, L.A. Grand Canyon
1961	56 Buick	moved - I went to Camp Martin Johnson, Baldwin, MI. My folks visited and drove around Lake Michigan.
1962	56 Buick	Utah , Colorado
1963	56 Buick	Mexico to San Cristobal de las Casas "Jiffy Buick" made it home & died at the car dealer when we went to get the new one - it was last seen being pushed away.
1964	61 Buick	Eastern Canada, Timmons, Ont, Montreal, Quebec, Gaspe.
1965	61 Buick	Tetons, Idaho, Oregon, Washington, Montana
1966	61 Buick	I danced at Parsons College, Fairfield, IA. Folks came and we went to Colorado, blew transmission near Sterling.
1967	61 Buick	Madison, IN, Lexington, KY, Smokies, Georgia, Florida, Key West, up the east coast to Washington, DC.
1968	61 Buick	Ohio, Pennsylvania, New York City, all of New England
1969	61 Buick	Colorado, Moab, Utah, Differential died
1970	61 Buick	Car died along the Oregon Trail 75 miles from Rock Springs, WY Monument Valley, Utah, Arizona, and Colorado.

Due to dad's condition my mother did all the driving until 1966 when I was finally old enough to drive legally. My dad loved photography. I have his collection of about 400 slides from each vacation. We would mail each roll of film in to get developed and when we got home we would be watching the slides from the first week or two of the trip before the car was even unloaded.

Unfortunately, as time went by he became less mobile but he still wanted to take the pictures. My mother and I became rather adapt at maneuvering the car into a position where he could take the picture. With the slower film speeds in those days the vibration of the car would cause blurred pictures so he always wanted us to turn the engine off. Back then, and with our cars, there was no guarantee that it would start again. Dad did not care if we were blocking traffic or risking our lives, he just wanted to get the best picture.

In 1959, dad wanted to drive down a canyon road along the Gunnison River in Colorado before they built a new dam that would block access. After driving a while we came upon a paper bag with the words ROCK SLIDE on a stick in the middle of the dirt road. So what does my dad say? "Go ahead, we can move them!"

Here was a man who could only walk with a cane and some assistance, traveling with his 5 foot one inch tall wife and a nine-year-old son saying, "We can move them."

After driving about five more miles we came upon the rock slide. Water was gurgling up around the rocks that were sticking up out of the roadway.

Mom had to back up for several miles until we came to a place where it was wide enough to try and turn the car around. My mother and I watched as a fisherman got in the car with dad and backed the rear of the car up the hill and then quickly turned it around. Dad was laughing and having a ball.

Had we been able to drive down the valley it would have been just another long boring drive but instead it is an example of the same spirit that drove a person who was told he would not be able to walk to open a dance studio.

Traveling 50 years ago was a bit different than now

Today, spending a month in a car would not appeal to most children. Life in the back seat of an old Buick was pretty nice especially since there were no seat belts, no car seats and no siblings.

Back then a "Camper" was a person who slept in a tent and not a huge vehicle that you drove or towed. A 1950s era sedan with a roof rack held more than a modern mini van or SUV. However, there were a few drawbacks since the old cars often overheated while going through the desert or had vapor locks while climbing a mountain. I don't miss having the heater going full blast trying to cool down the engine while we were driving around in the middle of the desert one bit.

On more than one occasion we had to tell mom where to steer as she tried to pull off the road after the roof rack slid down over the windshield while driving down a mountain road in the rain.

Freezing an arm off while holding onto a loose roof rack strap, while waiting for a place to pull off the road was another favorite pastime.

Before the "Americans with Disability Act" access to many places often depended upon a lot of ingenuity on the part of a family. We talked a guard into letting us drive our car up a service road so that dad could get next to Morning Glory Pool in Yellowstone National Park.

Wildlife Parks

Theme parks and wildlife parks were not major vacation destinations. Back then the west was a theme park. Wildlife roamed freely. Some would even come up to the car to be fed. Bears would walk through the campsites at both Yellowstone and Glacier National Parks.

Today, this photo would probably be labeled "Exhibit A" in a child endangerment lawsuit. Yes that is a bear.

Different Points of View

Just because another family member may have recorded their impressions of an event there is no reason not to also tell your side of the story as well. My mother kept a daily diary listing the towns that we had visited along with the starting mileage and some brief notes.

Part of the entry for one day says, "Chased sunset but missed Stopped at store." That evening I had stayed at the motel swimming. I waited and waited until well after dark for them to return so that we could go and eat dinner. The next day I drew a sketch of their adventure.

Dear, Let's just go over that hill for the sunset   **Just one more hill, Dear**

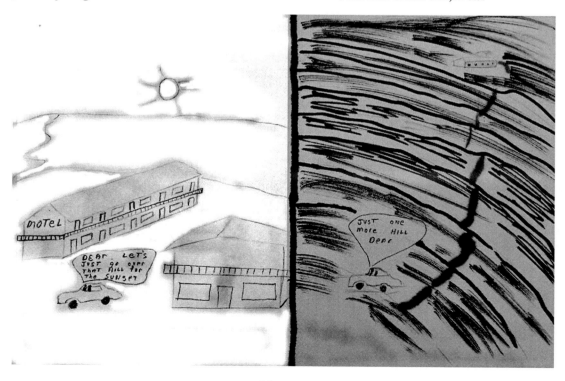

My dad loved sunsets. One of his hobbies was to see what strange out of the way places he could get us to drive to so that he could get the killer sunset photo. The only problem was the fact that once the sun sets, it's dark!

Unfortunately, we then needed to get back. One night I had to get out of our car and walk down the middle of a one lane mountain road lit only by our car's headlights so that my mother could follow me since she couldn't see the edge of the road.

Just like a fisherman with tales of the one that got away, we were driving back to the motel after having dinner at Niagara on the Lake when we saw the most spectacular sunset ever. It was then that we realized that the camera was back at the motel.

Early Family Life - The time period from when a couple first meet until their children are old enough to remember is the one that only they can really tell about.

One day when my mother was riding in the car with me she started telling about the first time that she saw my father and that it was "love at first sight." After I got back home I typed out what I remembered. She reviewed it and we made a few corrections.

On another occasion she told about performing when she was seven or eight months pregnant and at intermission I rolled over and all of a sudden she had a huge belly. Fortunately I rolled back and she was able to finish the performance. Needless to say they did not want any surprise guest appearances so that was her last performance for a while.

I was fortunate that my parents saved several newspaper articles about the opening of their new dance studio in the greystone (photo on the cover) that they were remodeling. The July 24, 1949 Chicago Daily Tribune had a two page article titled **Studio of Young Ballet Dancers Built in Jig Time** that included photographs of the home where I grew up. There were photographs of the studio with my father with a number of students. There were also photos of the living room and even one of my parents and me, two months before I was born. A copy of the article and photographs can be found at Proquest's Historical Chicago Tribune.

In 2011 I scanned most of the photographs that we had from the time that I first met my wife until

the twins were about eight years old. It included all of our houses, the boys as babies and young children, our pets, a number of birthday parties and Christmas gatherings.

I also included historical and current photos of our home. I arranged them by date and put them on digital media.

After looking at them the twins observed that their older bother smiled a lot more before they were born!

Organizing It All

Before long there will be a number of forms, supporting documents, photos, and stories. A little basic organization will help you manage all of this information.

Start with a heavy-duty three-ring binder. When the project is completed you may want to purchase a higher quality binder that can be displayed.

Within the notebook you will want to have dividers and arrange the information as follows:

1. Cover Sheet – Include a Title or Family Name, an inscription, your name and the date.

2. Ancestor Chart(s)

3. Family Names – with an Index Tab for each Family
   They can be in alphabetical order or follow the order of the Ancestor Chart.
   Included should be:
   - Family Group Sheets (FGS) from newest to oldest
   - Individual Timelines & Stories following the FGS where the person is a parent
   - Copies of Supporting Information:
       Birth, Marriage, and Death Records, Documents, or Newspaper Articles
   - Copies of Photographs with the people identified

Getting Started

If you just want to document your family, preserve the home sources, and begin recording your family's stories then you can start by filling in the forms in the "Our Family" section at the back of the book.

To see how the information that you found and compiled can be used to help research your family or to find out how to obtain those missing certificates you can read or at least review the following "Family History Research" section.

Maybe you are not that interested right now. You can always come back and read it at a later date when you want to get the answers to a few questions or you decide that you really want to find out more about your family's history.

Family History Research

After filling in the forms with what you remembered and from the facts that you found in the various home sources you might be curious about some of the missing names, dates or places.

Maybe you just want to find out a little more about Grandpa or some other relative, congratulations, you just found yourself joining the growing number of people doing family history research. Having filled out the various forms and gathered the various home sources you are off to a great start.

So, What are the Next Steps?

The first thing to remember is to **Work from Known to Unknown!** Start with yourself and prove that your parents are your parents and then keep working backwards. Do not rely upon anyone else's research. Use it as a clue that still needs to be verified if there are no supporting documents.

Do not be afraid to **Use the Internet.** There are a wide variety of internet sites that can help you with your research. Access to all of the free websites listed in this book can be found at www.JeffBockman.com and then choose **Genealogy & Travel Links**. Select the desired topic from the list on the left and the links will appear on the right side. Since internet addresses change frequently, few are listed in the book. Suggested topics will be shown as {topic: ?}.

If you do not have internet access then ask at your local library. Most offer internet access and many also offer free access to Ancestry Library Edition, Heritage Quest Online, Newspaper archives, and many other genealogical research tools. FamilySearch.org is a free internet site. Some hints about searching the internet can be found in the "If you Didn't Find it in the Index" section on page 42.

If you haven't already done so, then **Contact Other Relatives,** especially any older ones to see what they remember and to get copies of any home sources that they might have. If you have lost contact with someone then use Google or any number of the online telephone directories {topic: Telephone} to try and locate them. Searching Google by their "name, city, state" may bring up their address and phone number. Enter their old phone number to see if it is still their number.

Not sure if someone is still alive? Check the Social Security Death Index {topic: Death} to see if they have died. If so then locate an obituary to find their living family members.

Vital Records

Start by trying to obtain any missing Birth, Death, and Marriage Certificates for your immediate family and the people that you want to research.

The information captured on a certificate, the date that they began keeping records, and access to records will vary greatly depending upon the jurisdiction. A jurisdiction is the geographical area over which a court or government body has the power and right to exercise authority.

- ➤ In New England (Connecticut, Rhode Island, Massachusetts, New Hampshire, Vermont, and Maine) it is usually the town.
- ➤ In most other places it is the county and the County Clerk keeps the records.
- ➤ Record access in some states is now handled by the state government.

Use Everton Publishers' *The Handybook for Genealogists* or the USGenWeb Project to see when a particular town or county started to keep records and where they are kept.

Go to the USGenWeb Project {topic: GenWeb} and select the desired state. At the state GenWeb page you can learn about any statewide resources and then select the desired county. The county site may help you learn what records are available and how to obtain them. The content varies greatly at these volunteer sites.

Indexes or even digital copies of older records may be available online. Check FamilySearch and Ancestry and then search the internet for the state, county and the type of record. If you find a record be sure to "Save" the image to your computer with a descriptive name in a known location.

Check the jurisdiction's website to verify the current rules and prices for obtaining records since they change frequently. There may be an online ordering method or a form to print out and mail in with the payment. Check to see if there is a genealogical copy available. They usually cost much less than a certified copy.

The information recorded on a certificate will vary greatly by jurisdiction. It may also vary for different time periods within the same jurisdiction. The following information is usually included:

Birth Certificate:

> Primary: Baby's Name, Date and Place of Birth, Mother's name and age.
> Secondary: Father's name and age, parent's birth place and most other information

Marriage Records

> Application for a Marriage License – It is not always available, but try to obtain one.
>> Contains valuable secondary information on birth, parents, and occupations.
> License to get married
>> Usually contains only their names and the date that the license was issued.
>> Might include their ages and the name of a parent if one was a minor.
> Certificate returned after the marriage ceremony
>> Usually just their names, date of marriage, and the official that married them
>> May include their parents names, witnesses, and other information.

Death Certificate:

> Primary: Name, date, place, and cause of death, funeral home, and cemetery.
> Secondary: Possibly birth date, place of birth, address, occupation, parent's names.
>> It can provide a lot of clues especially if the informant was knowledgeable.

The **Quality of Information** will depend upon a number of things. Who originally provided the information and how knowledgeable were they? How was it recorded? What is the condition of the original record?

Some requested certificates are a copy of the original while others are a typed or handwritten version. Copies of an original document may include a person's signature, which can help to differentiate between two people with the same name. Typed or handwritten versions have a greater opportunity for transcription errors.

Vital Record Indexes

If the location of an event is unknown there are a number of online indexes that might help. Since most of them cover a limited time period or a selected area, be sure to review the "about the website" section for every database to see what records, location, and date ranges are included.

Deaths: {topic: Death} The Social Security Death Index. (SSDI) is the only countrywide index and it covers only the deaths of those people that were collecting Social Security benefits and died between 1965 and a few months ago. There are a variety of state and county death indexes online. Older certificate images have been posted by some jurisdictions and FamilySearch.

Marriages: {topic: Marriage} There is no nationwide index. The various statewide and countywide indexes vary greatly. Some sites like Clark County, Nevada show the official data on marriages from 1984 to yesterday. Others are volunteer projects like the IL Marriage Records prior to 1901 that is missing entries for several counties and the time periods vary for many of the others.

Births: {topic: Birth} The birth date, but not their parent's names can be found for many living people at Birthdatabase.com. FamilySearch has posted some older county birth registers online and are indexing them. A few other state indexes are available for the late 1800s and early 1900s.

Other Vital Record Indexes - There are many books and electronic databases that contain extracts or indexes of vital records. The Barbour Collection contains early Connecticut town records. There is a series of books with Massachusetts town records up to 1850. To see if there are any books for a particular area search WorldCat {topic: Library}, an online library catalog that can tell you if there is a book and the closest library that has it. Also check Google Books and BYU Family History Archive {topic: Books} for a digital version to view and download.

No Birth Certificate!

It may be impossible to obtain a birth certificate for some people since access to birth certificates is being restricted in many states to births over 75 to 100 years ago and the fact that many places did not start keeping birth records until after 1900 to 1933. Don't be discouraged.

Remember that you are not looking to "certify" that they were born. You know that they had to have been born if they lived, had children, died or were buried. You are only looking for a few key details about their birth and trying to find and prove a connection to their parents.

➤ **Date of Birth** - Their birth date would be on their Naturalization papers or those of their spouse or a parent. It would be on their death certificate or tombstone if the informant was informed.

It is possible to use the ages that were given on a number of other records to narrow down the range of someone's birth date. The example below shows how the range for the birth date of Alvar Bockman was narrowed down to between December 21, 1890 and February 24, 1891 by taking the latest low date and the earliest high date. His age in the census record was incorrect.

Event	Date	Age	Low Date	High Date
Wedding	05-13-1917	26	5/14/1890	5/13/1891
Birth #1	06-17-1918	27	6/18/1890	6/17/1891
Census	01-01-1920	27	~~1/2/1892~~	~~1/1/1893~~
Birth #2	02-25-1920	29	2/26/1890	**2/25/1891**
Birth #3	12-20-1921	30	**12/21/1890**	12/20/1891
Birth #4	05-21-1925	34	5/22/1890	5/21/1891

Low Birth Date assumes his birthday will be tomorrow and the age will increase.
High Birth Date assumes that today was his birthday and the age just changed.

Alvar's Jan. 25, 1891 date of birth was eventually found. See "Finding Alvar" on page 48.

- **Place of Birth**: A child's birth certificate will usually list their parent's place of birth either the state or country while others may have the exact town. A person's death certificate may list their place of birth if the informant knew it. Immigration and Naturalization records asked for the person's place of birth. The 1917 WWI and 1942 WWII Draft Registration cards asked for both their birth date and place. Census records show a person's state or country of birth.

- **Parents** – Finding a person's parents and linking to prior generations is one of the goals of family history research. The following records can help to connect a person with their parents either by providing possible names or by actually providing proof: census records, a death certificate, newspaper stories & obituaries, tombstones, cemetery records, or even by them just being buried together. A person's SS-5 Social Security Application lists their parent's names.

  Records created by a possible parent can then often provide the proof. Probate records list all of the living children. Naturalization papers list the person's children along with their date and place of birth. US Census records, after 1880, show the relationship to the head of household.

Records to Help Find or Prove a Person's Parents

Wills & Probate Records

A will is document that the person created to tell how they would like to have their estate handled after their death. They were often filed at the courthouse and transcribed into Will Books. Some give very detailed accounts of their property and land holdings along with instructions on what everyone should receive. Many include the name of the wife and a list of all of the living children including the daughter's married names and occasionally even their spouse's name. Unfortunately some just state that I leave everything to "my wife."

Probate Records are all of the records related to the disposition of an estate after a person's death. The jurisdiction is usually the County Probate Court. An estate will be probated where the person lived at the time of their death and also in any other jurisdiction where the decedent owned property. The legal proceeding can provide a number of interesting and useful records including:

- Petition or Application – This form starts a probate case where the person did not leave a will. It includes a listing of the people, usually the wife and children, with a claim on the estate and their current locations.
- Announcements – Legal notices are then published in various newspapers in the towns where the family and other creditors are located.
- Court Proceedings – transcripts of the case.
- Listing of Assets – a detailed list of all of the deceased's property
- Proof of Claim – Supporting documents for a debt or to prove the person's relationship.
- Affidavits – Statements made under oath about their relationship and claim.
- Distribution of Assets – Court orders on who was to receive what assets.
- Receipts: Monument Company, Cemetery, Funeral Home, and Debtors
    (These are all clues to other records)

The County Clerk or Probate Court usually has the Will Books that contain the transcribed versions of the wills ordered by the year and the date recorded. There is usually an index in the front of each volume. Sometimes there is also an Index to Wills.

Access to Probate Indexes and Records will vary greatly by jurisdiction. Many older index books are available to the general public. In some areas the clerk must look it up. More recent probate indexes are often on computers. In some jurisdictions access to the physical files is restricted but in others you can climb up the movable steps, pull out the four inch wide file drawer, and look through the file that contains all of the various documents.

In some jurisdictions the probate cases are filed with other court cases. There was at least a Preliminary Hearing and a Final Hearing. At the end of the preliminary hearing they will set the date for the final hearing. If the name is not found in the index then look by the court date.

There are many published Lists and Abstracts of older wills. Some are by county while others may be for a surname. Search Worldcat by the location and wills or will book. Try searching the internet for a person's name and will. I have found many early 1800 Campbell County Virginia wills online.

Cemetery Records

A person's death certificate or obituary will usually list the cemetery where they were buried. Contact or visit the cemetery office to find out who purchased the burial plot and to see who else is buried in it. Do not just rely on reading the tombstones. People can be buried without having a tombstone. Memorial tombstones can be placed without someone actually being buried there. Multiple people can be buried in a single grave and there may only be a headstone for one of them. To find out what is really below the ground, you need to see the cemetery records.

People are often buried with members of their family or their in-laws. Occasionally people are buried in single plots or in another family's plot when there are no more living family members. Even if the other names in the plot are not familiar and the cemetery records do not explain the relationships you should still get the names and death dates of everyone in the plot, they might be related. Try to find the obituaries for everyone since they often give some family relationships that may help to tie the various people together.

Newspaper Obituaries

Modern obituaries often contain considerable information about the deceased including everything from their grandparents to their grandchildren, schools attended, places of employment, any major accomplishments or awards, along with the various towns where they previously lived.

Older obituaries contained much less information unless the person was famous. They might still provide the information that can help to link generations. A single obituary may contain errors or give only a small amount of information. Check for other obituaries, death notices, news stories and society news for several days after the death. Additional information or corrections may be printed in the other editions or on another day. Look for articles published prior to the death, especially if it was caused by an accident. Also check for stories about distant family members coming to town or about the church members helping the family if it was a prolonged illness.

The following obituaries helped to tie several generations of the Demary/West/ Rayworth Family together. They are all buried in a single plot at the Rosehill Cemetery in Chicago, Illinois.

- Nov 22, 1867 Chicago Tribune – DIED - In this city, Nov. 21st 1867 at the residence of her daughter (Mrs. H.H. Demary) 241 Warren St, Mrs Esther West, aged 80 years and 6 months. Funeral from residence today (Friday) at 12 noon."

- Oct 10, 1899 Chicago Tribune – DEATHS - De Mary - Oct 9, 1899 Hiram H. De Mary in his 85th year. Funeral private, Denver and Leadville Colo papers please copy"
- Oct 12, 1899 Chicago Tribune - DEATH RECORD BURIAL PERMIT ISSUED - "De Mary H. H. 84 Home for Incurables Oct 9"

- June 18, 1905 Chicago Sunday Tribune DEATHS - "**DeMavy - Mrs. Jane** June 17 in her 91st year. Mother of Edward M. Raworth, Kate Reworth Holmes and Helen E. Stevenson. "
- June 19, 1905 Chicago Tribune – DEATHS - "DeMary - the funeral of **Mrs. Jane De Mary** will take place from the residence of her daughter Mrs. D.M. Stevenson 170 36th St. Tuesday June 20 at 10 a.m. to Rosehill by car. Burial private."
- June 20, 1905 Chicago Tribune – DEATHS - "**De Mary Jane** 90 170 36th St. June 17"

- Dec. 30, 1914 Chicago Daily Tribune - OBITUARY (page 7 column 1) "**Mrs. Helen E. Stevenson** wife of Donald Stevenson died yesterday at . . . residence 536 East Thirty Sixth Street. She was born in Alexander, NY in 1851 and came to Chicago when a girl. She was one of the organizers of the Camera Club and later its president. She is survived by her husband Donald, and two sons. Funeral service will be held at the late residence tomorrow afternoon. Burial at Rosehill."
- Dec. 30, 1914 Chicago Daily Tribune - DEATHS (page 15 column 5) "STEVENSON - **Helen E. Stevenson**, wife of Donald M. Stevenson, at her home, 536 E. 30th St., yesterday afternoon. Funeral 2 o'clock Thursday. Denver papers please copy.

- Jan. 23, 1922 Chicago Daily Tribune - DEATH NOTICES - "Stevenson - **Donald M. Stevenson** Jan 22 in his seventy-seventh year. Two sons surviving, Raworth W. Stevenson and John G. Stevenson. Funeral from Rosehill chapel on Tuesday at 2 o'clock in the afternoon."

Notices for other papers to "please copy" are a clue that either the person once lived there or that a family member currently lives there. Hiram spent most of his life in Leadville and Helen's half sister Kate Holmes lived in Denver.

Census Records

Census records are a great tool for verifying a known family relationship or to actually discover the parents and siblings of a person. The census records from 1850 to 1940 list everyone living in a household so that children can be found living with their parents and then in later years a now older parent can often be found living in the home of one of their children. The information recorded for an individual can often lead the researcher to other helpful records.

Census records can often be difficult to read due to poor handwriting on the part of the census taker or due to damaged or faded records. Some of the information may be confusing or just plain wrong. In spite of these apparent problems, census records are a great research tool and should be used.

One thing to keep in mind is the question "**Why were the US Census records collected?**" The answer is contained in a Constitutional provision:

> "Representatives and direct Taxes shall be apportioned among the several states ... according to their respective Numbers... The actual Enumeration shall be made within three Years after the first Meeting of the Congress of the United States and within every subsequent Term of ten Years, in such Manner as they shall by Law direct."
> *Art. 1, Sec. 2*

The census taker or enumerator was being paid to "Count The People." They went house to house and talked to whomever they could to get the information about who lived in each household. It could have been the head of the household, the spouse, a child, a parent, an in-law, a boarder, or possibly even just a neighbor.

Please remember that they were only being paid to "**count the people**" and not to obtain documented genealogical evidence for descendants one or two hundred years later!

The census was taken every ten years beginning in 1790. The questions asked changed almost every time and often reflected changes in the country at the time. There was a major change in 1850 when they began to record detailed information on everyone living in a household and not just recording the name of the head of the household and how many people of different ages and sex lived there.

Key Information in the US Census Records

1790 - 1840	Name of Head of Household, Counts by age group and category: Free White Males, Free White Females, Slaves, All Other (Free Colored, Foreigner, etc.)
1850 - 1860	**Names of everyone**, **Age**, **Sex**, Color, Occupation, Value Real Estate, Personal Property, **Birthplace**, **Married within Year**, School within Year.
1870	Same as 1860 with **Father Foreign born**, **Mother Foreign born**, Month born in year, Month married in year, Eligible to vote, Insane or Idiotic.
1880	Same plus **Relationship to Head of House**, Single, Married, Widowed, Divorced, **Place of Birth**, **Father's Place of Birth**, **Mother's Place of Birth**. Street Number and Name in Cities.
1890	Most of the 1890 Census records were lost in a fire.
1900	Household members as of June 1, 1900 **Month of Birth, Year of Birth, Number of years Married, Mother of how many children, Number of these children living , Year of Immigration to the US, Number of years in US., Naturalization, Home owned or rented**, Owned free or mortgage.
1910	Household members as of April 15, 1910 No Birth month or year, **Number of years present marriage**, **Native language**, Trade, **Union or Confederate Veteran**.
1920	Household members as of January 1, 1920 **Year of Naturalization, Mother Tongue of Father, and Mother**, No information on the number of children.
1930	Household members as of April 1, 1930 **Age at first marriage**, Own a radio, **Veteran of which war**, Unemployed
1940	Household members as of April 1, 1940 Value of home or **amount of rent, Highest grade of school, Where lived 4/1/1935** Questions about employment & government work, seeking job, **Salary in 1939**.

Finding & Viewing Census Records

The easiest method of finding and viewing the US Census Records is by using Ancestry or Heritage Quest Online census collections. Free access is available at a variety of libraries. Both collections contain all of the census images however the indexes at Ancestry include "everyone" while H.Q. Online is missing indexes for several years and others include only the head of household. Even an "every name" index does not always find everyone. FamilySearch has free indexes for all years and images for 1900 and 1940. Be sure to save the census images to your computer or storage device using a descriptive name (ex: 1850 VA Campbell Western p23) in a known file location.

Census Online – {topic: Census} has links by State and County to a variety of census records. Some are actual images while others are indexes or transcribed records.

Microfilm Collections – Microfilmed versions of all census records and the available soundex indexes are available at NARA (National Archives & Record Administration) facilities and at most major genealogy libraries. Local or partial collections are available at many local research facilities.

Research Strategy

Remember to work from known to unknown. For people with a common name it will be easier if you can start searching the state or city where you know that they were living at the time. Knowing their age or approximate year of birth will help to narrow down the choices but don't be too exact since the ages given were not always correct and the age doesn't always translate into the correct year. For those people with a unique name, search by the name and then narrow it down further if necessary.

When trying to find someone's parents search a single census when they would be a young child normally living at home. Knowing the names of any siblings will help to identify the correct family. If the person was born after the census was taken then knowing the older siblings can help to find the family. Check the later census records to see if one of the parents might be living with them. The birthplace of the mother and father can also help to identify possible parents.

With the online records it is now fairly easy to obtain all of the census records for the years between 1940 and 1850. Like an Olympic judge you may need to throw out the high and low replies and average the rest to determine the probable correct answer.

Making Sense of the Information

The enumeration dates varied from census to census so a person's age may not always be just 10 years more. There may be a reason that the age changed. Maybe the person answering the questions didn't really know the person's age or perhaps they married someone much younger or older and they didn't want it to appear that there was that much of a difference.

The "Relationship to the Head of Household" began in 1880. This showed that a child was the son or daughter of the head. It does not mean that they were the children of the listed wife. The child's birthplace of the mother could help to differentiate mothers if there were more than one spouse and they were born in different states. The number of years married, married within the year, how many children, and how many are living can also help to show if the wife is or is not the mother.

Sometimes it is possible to tell who gave the information based upon apparently incorrect answers recorded by the census taker. The wife was usually at home and often the person answering the questions. She might have said that a person living with them was her mother. The recorded answer occasionally was "mother" rather than being correctly translated into "mother-in-law." If the relationships do not appear to be correct for the head then see if they make sense for the spouse.

Occasionally you can almost interpret the person's feeling and hear them say that "that lady is my mother-in-law and that the two girls living with them are her daughters." The census taker should have changed the relationships to the head of the household as mother and sisters rather than showing the girls as daughters that were only a few years younger than the head.

If you come across incorrect or conflicting information on a single census record remember that anyone could have provided the information or the person may have "adjusted" the answer for any number of reasons. Review several census records to see if there is a consensus of information.

Clues to Other Records

The answers to various census questions can help lead a researcher to other records. Questions about Immigration and Naturalization let you know that there were other records created. When a year is listed or they answer questions like "how long ago" that helps you narrow down the time frame for a search. Answers can also show if there should be military, land, or mortgage records. If some of the children were born in different states then their migration path and the time periods becomes apparent.

Census records are a clue to other records

Clues from Column Titles	1850	1860	1870	1880	1900	1910	1920	1930	1940	Other Records
Birthday										Vital/Church records
Name, Sex and Age	x	x	x	x	x	x	x	x	x	Year (+/- 1)
Birthplace/Place of Birth	x	x	x	x	x	x	x	x	x	Location
Month & Year of Birth					x					Month & Year
Census Year Month of Birth			x	x						Month if 1870 or 80
Marriage										
Married within Census Year	x	x	x	x						Year if 1850, 60, 70, 80
Number of Years Married					x					Year
No. Years Present Marriage						x				Year
Married?							x	x	x	Shows Relationship
Immigration - Person										
Birthplace	x	x	x	x	x	x	x	x	x	If not US.
Year of Immigration					x	x	x	x		When
Number of Years in US.					x					(silly question ?)
Naturalized or Alien					x	x	x	x	x	Records if Naturalized
Immigration - Parents										Immigration Records
Father Foreign Born			x							Possible Immigrant
Father's Place of Birth				x	x	x	x	x	s	Location
Father's Mother Tongue						x				Location
Mother Foreign Born			x							Possible Immigrant
Mother's Place of Birth				x	x	x	x	x	s	Location
Mother's Mother Tongue						x				Location
Land Ownership										Land Records
Home Owned/Rented					x	x	x	x	x	Land, Tax Records
Owned free or mortgage					x	x	x			Land Records
Street Address				x	x	x	x	x	x	Land Records
Value Real Estate/Per Prop.	R	R+P	R+P					x	x	Land, Tax Records
Occupation										
Occupation	x	x	x	x	x	x	x	x	x	Directories, Company
Military Service										
Union or Confederate Vet.						x		Vet	s	Military Records
Family										
Relationship to head of fam.				x	x	x	x	x	x	
Number Children & Living					x	x				

Other Records

After obtaining the vital records, reading any newspaper stories and obituaries, reviewing cemetery records and tombstones, obtaining the wills & probate records, and then finding the census records there are still many other types of records that can help you in your family history research.

Consider attending genealogy classes or lectures to learn about the various records that can help you with your research and also about researching any specific ethnic groups and foreign countries.

Family Bible	Some family bibles are in online historical and library collections. Individuals have also posted images or transcribed bibles {Bible}
Biographical Sketches	Narratives about a family's history {topic: Books}
Church Records	Created for: christenings or baptisms, marriages, funerals, burials
City Directories	Books that list everyone living in the town along with businesses
Telephone Directories	These list everyone in the town with a telephone
Divorce	Records are usually with the county clerk, there are some online indexes. The records usually list any children.
Family Books	Published family histories – check WorldCat.com to locate them at local libraries or search for them online. {topic: Books}
Land	County Courthouses have grantor (seller) and grantee (buyer) indexes
Local Histories	Town or County History books tell about the area where your family lived. They start out with the first settlers, clearing the land, the first businesses, who founded the various churches and schools. Many also include biographical sketches and images of the more prominent or wealthy citizens. They usually paid for their inclusion. {topic: Books}
Maps/Atlases	Old county atlases and plat maps show the landowners, Sandborn Fire Insurance maps show the construction of city buildings, Both help to learn about the neighbors and neighborhood. Topographical maps show the features of the land including cemeteries. Historical maps show jurisdictional boundaries. Google maps can locate and display satellite images of cemeteries. {topic: Maps & Historical Maps}
Military Records	World War I and World War II draft cards are available at Ancestry. World War II Army enlistments and military cemetery burials are also online. There are published regimental histories, Revolutionary War Pension Files, Civil War causalities, and more. {topic: Military}
Newspapers	Newspapers can provide additional details on a known event and provide an insight into the time and place where they were living. Search WorldCat.com by the town's name and "newspapers" to find a physical or microfilm collection and the closest library where they can be viewed. Obituaries and other stores are available online at many commercial and historical websites. Some like Colorado Historical Newspapers are "every word searchable" and include images of the articles. {topic: Newspapers}

Immigrants

Many foreign civil and church records are now available online. Unfortunately most of them are not indexed. In order to view either the actual or online records you need to know the town or parish.

If you have not found the exact date and place of birth you have hopefully been able to narrowed it down. Look for clues to their hometown in the following sources and records: Family Sources including any correspondence, Oral History & Stories, Local Histories & Biographical Sketches, their Children's Birth Certificates, WWI and WWII Draft Registration, their SS Application, their Military Records, Newspaper stories, and the various Death Records if the informant knew it.

Coming to America

Immigrants have been coming to North America and staying since 1620. The records and availability vary greatly depending up the time period and the country of departure.

The 1900 to 1940 US census records show the year of arrival and if they have been naturalized. The 1920 census provides the year of naturalization. The language spoken in the home and the language of the parents can help to narrow down their area of origin. For immigrants that left Austria before WWI knowing that they spoke German, Slovenian, Hungarian, or another language is very helpful.

Emigration Records	Departure registration or permission and passports issued from their country of origin or the country of departure.
Passenger Lists	Indexes for various time periods are available in print. Ancestry and other sites have posted many passenger lists or indexes online. There may be a different list at both the port of departure and arrival. Abbreviations and initials were often used instead of full first names.
Immigration	Immigration Records and Customs lists. The Ellis Island and Castle Garden websites provide information on New York City arrivals. Ancestry and FamilySearch have records for many other ports. Microfilms of port records are available at National Archive facilities and some are available for viewing at FamilySearch Centers.
Naturalization	Naturalization Papers: The Declaration of Intent and the Petition For Citizenship both provide information on their spouse and children. Before 1906 the records were filed at local courthouses. After 1906 the federal courts handled them and the papers are at NARA.
Still stuck?	If the desired information or records for your ancestor cannot be located, then look for the records of their parents, spouse, and any siblings. Their records may contain more information.
Really stuck?	Check the records of: Witnesses on their marriage certificate or other records; Neighbors in the census records that were from the same country. They may be from the same town or area.

Research Hints & Stories

The following section contains: Research lessons and online searching hints; Genealogical travel examples including walking in my grandfather's footprints in France; and concludes with a case study about finding out what happened to my other grandfather Alvar and discovering his parents.

If you Didn't Find it in the Index,
It only means that you "Didn't Find it in the Index!"

This was one of the first lessons that I learned after starting to do genealogical research.

My maternal grandfather John Stevenson could not be found in the 1920 soundex index. Now he cannot be found in any of the online indexes. The soundex card for the household showed his family's last name as Johnston, dittos of the head of the household, Granville Johnston, John's father-in-law. In the actual record the last name of John, his wife, and daughter were blank.

Another example was an index of court and probate records in a western New York state courthouse that did not show the second probate hearing. After searching several books for the second or third time, I heard my wife say, "What if it isn't in the index?" Sure enough the case was recorded correctly by date but it had not been entered in the index. The clerk then wrote the 1859 entry in the index, over one hundred and forty years later.

A third example was a Triplett Family book that had been revised to include three additional generations including my parents who were incorrectly shown as Boekman. Unfortunately the index at the back of the book was not updated to include the additional generations.

Online Information

The good news is that there is tremendous amount of digitized information now available on the internet and it is growing daily. The bad news is that online sources have similar problems. People expect that everything a computer does is correct. It only does what it is programmed to do with the information that was entered. Do you always get what you expected? Not always is probably a pretty fair answer.

Detectives often follow the money to solve a crime. You should try to "Follow the Data" and also learn a little bit about it. Learn why a record was created and what was included. See who provided the information and who recorded it. Do the same for any indexes. If the data was not that important to the recorder then that may help to explain some of the inconsistencies. There can also be issues with the legibility and readability of the records even when they were recorded correctly.

Online Indexes can also have problems. The images and the handwriting can be difficult to read. Are the people doing the indexing paid contractors rewarded for quantity or volunteers hopefully striving for quality. Are they familiar with the local names, terms, forms, and handwriting?

Optical Character Recognition, OCR is often used to index printed sources such as newspapers, books, and other publications. The software can easily misinterpret letters if a fancy or enlarged font is used or if there is a distorted image. Typesetters often used alternative pieces of type if they ran out of the correct letter. (vv instead of a w). Individuals will read it as desired but the computer won't. An extreme example is in a book where "B. Werner" is on the top of every even page. The result was a wide variety of spellings and only about 20% of the time was it correct!

Searching Online Information

All of the mega genealogy sites encourage access by a person's name. This may be helpful for those with a unique first or last name and for your "Brickwall" people. It is probably not the best method for those people with a common name or one that is often misspelled.

Search the individual databases where there is a high probability of a record rather than the entire site. Use additional criteria to further reduce the number of records to a manageable number.

Many of the database titles appear to be all inclusive but the content often is not. Look at the detailed description to see what records, locations, and time periods are included.

Search for all of the names of the primary people in an event. Search for the bride and groom separately if not found at first. Also try her maiden and any other married names. Search for all of their other spouses and try various spellings if necessary.

For those names that are often misspelled use wildcards for either a single character or for several characters. Check the website to see what characters they utilize and the conditions for their use. Ancestry.com requires at least three characters to use a wildcard and you cannot start and end with a wildcard. Use a wildcard in place of special foreign language characters if it not automatically done.

Still Not Getting the Desired Results

Does the question on a query form match the data? The census record has the person's age while most online searches ask for the birth year. You need to use "+/- 1" year for many searches to return the correct result even when the correct age was recorded.

Is the data field included in the index? For ten years a search of Ancestry's 1930 Census by a child's birth place would not get any results. It was only indexed for the "head of household." This was corrected in 2012.

Learn about the data and its format. Find any record (use "Smith") to review the displayed fields, the entered data, and the format of the entries. Do they use full names, abbreviated first names, or just initials? Many passenger lists do not have everyone's full name. Pick any record and then try searching for it using the same terms as your attempted query to see if it works .

Do Not Stop at the Index! View the Actual Image! I cannot stress this enough. Review the search results but do not dismiss a record of interest without looking at the actual record. I have seen indexes that showed PA for Panama and DE for Denmark. An arrival date of the "1st" was displayed as "14." If you cannot find someone from Denmark then search for Delaware.

If you didn't find it in the Index - BROWSE! When you are unable to find anything in the index, narrow things down by category, location, or time period and then browse the records.

Gold in them thar Online Books

Even with the noted OCR problems, online books, newspapers, and publications can provide information that may not otherwise be found. Biographical sketches, county histories, and family books can contain a wealth of information. They were often not indexed or were poorly indexed. Online books can be found at: Google Books, BYU Family History Archive, and HeritageQuest Online (via library access). Some claim that every word is indexed but I have had problems locating a page after searching by the names or terms found on a prior printout. You can often search within a publication but also read the book and index as you would a printed book.

Online Historical Newspapers are available at many sites. You never know what you will find in a newspaper, but you will find nothing if you do not look! Start with where they were born, married, died or were living in the census years. You might even locate articles in places where you would never have considered looking. Newspapers carried stories from other cities that were sensational or of world or local interest. Do not be afraid to search the New York Times or any other good online paper even if your family never lived there. Remember that "Name Searches" are just searching the text and articles may have used a person's nickname or an abbreviation. Searching by names may find surprising stories while at the same time not return some that you would have expected.

Trouble Finding an Online Article? There is nothing more frustrating than having a copy of an article or knowing the date and place of an event and not being able to locate anything. Unfortunately every word in every story is not always indexed or indexed correctly! If you are looking for a specific event try to search by the date and a column's title or topic. If that does not work than enter a date and the paper's name. Select any article, then switch to the full page view and review the entire page. Then review each page in the entire newspaper. You can download all of the pages for several days around the time of an event and then review them later. Column titles are usually indexed while all of the contents are not.

Publicity for one site showed that 1890 was now online. I looked for an April 1890 article and did not find it. I searched for "Marine News" and 1890 and sorted the results from oldest to newest. The first issue shown was in June. I waited several months for the beginning of the year to be posted.

Is Every Page Included? After finding a particular date I knew that something was wrong when there were only seven pages listed instead of the normal eight for the weekday paper. The link for page 4 went to the actual page 5. The real Page 4, the one I wanted, was missing. I eventually found it in another collection.

I searched GenealogyBank for information in the *New Orleans Times Picayune* about an Edward Neuhaus who had arrived on the Suldal on June 30, 1900 and I did not find any results. I searched for "Marine News" on June 30th and there listed under Steamers in the "List of Vessels in Port, June 30, 1890" was the "Suldal - Bluefields - 1st district 15." On the same page was an article "From Nicaragua" that told about the voyage of the Suldal and how it had arrived on the 28th and docked on the 29[th.] It listed the two cabin passengers, Edward Neuhaus and Frank Abbott. The ship's name did look like Suidal. On page 7 was "The Hotels - Record of Yesterday's Arrivals" which showed that "Ed Newhaus, Nicaragua" had checked into the Commercial Hotel. Even though the search for Neuhaus in June 1900 returned no entries, there were two articles about him.

If you didn't find it in the Index - Read the Paper! Sometimes great family information is buried in personal ads, business advertisements, social news, and the many other small stories that often do not get fully indexed. Review an entire weekday paper and a Sunday paper to see what was normally included. They were often only four to twelve pages long, sometimes up to twenty in a larger city. Each newspaper has a unique focus and areas of interest.

The 1890s the *New Orleans Times Picayune* contained considerable information about marine activities including people and cargo on both the sea and the Mississippi River. Visitors and regional businesses were also covered. While looking for information about a May 1890 marriage, I found their names in the "Vital Statistics" column that listed the marriages recorded the previous day. Looking for an article about the wedding I noticed that a "Personal & General Notes" column listed the names of the people who had checked into the major downtown hotels on the prior day. I backed up a few days and found out when they arrived in town and which hotel they each stayed at.

By contrast the 1892 *Boston Times* contained more stories about local people and activities, such as yacht and bicycle races, than information on visitors to the city and non-European ship arrivals. The merchant ship arrival that I was looking for was eventually found in the *Boston Daily Advertiser*.

Expectations & Reality Indexes are just the "Tip of the Iceberg." Most do not cover every word on every page. Even if they did there are bound to be errors. However, being able to find records, publications, and newspapers online by either searching or browsing is wonderful.

Remember "**If you didn't find it in the index, it only means that you didn't find it in the index!**"

Genealogy Travel

As you have read, travel has been a major part of my life. Today it still plays an important role helping me to learn more about my family's history. Even with all of the information and records on the internet there are still many reasons to travel to the places where your family lived.

Research

All records are not online. Even if the vital records are online, probate and land records will still probably require a courthouse visit. A visit to the cemetery is needed to view all of the records, see the plot, gather information on everyone buried nearby, and to view the stones.

The feeling I got from standing at the 300 year old grave of my 7th Great Grandfather Lt. Thomas Miner cannot be duplicated by looking at photos.

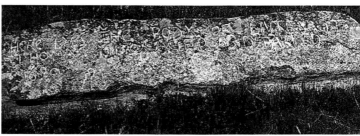
Here Lies the Body of Lieutenant Thomas Miner died 1690

Local libraries and research centers will often have resources that are only available there. Being able to talk with the people who are familiar with the area, its history, and the records can be very interesting and save you a lot of time. Developing a congenial relationship with the people who control access to the records can also be very beneficial.

Walking in your Ancestor's Footsteps

Visiting the country, the town, or possibly even the house where an ancestor was born, lived or just spent time is an experience that cannot be done online. Learning about their culture, sampling the food, and enjoying the local beverages of choice can help you connect with your ancestors and maybe even living cousins. Finding a local family member or even an interested contact can make it a very special experience.

Here are a few examples of my travels to family sites that were enhanced by local contacts:

Slovenia: In 1999 Eva, a relative from Slovenia replied to a query that I had posted. In 2000 my wife and I went to Slovenia and met Eva and her parents in Ljubljana. They translated for us when we met 19 cousins in the village where my father's mother was born and grew up. We really enjoyed meeting them, the food, and their homemade wine and slivovitz (plum brandy).

Colorado: Hiram DeMary, a Great-Great Grandfather helped Colorado become a state and he spent much of his life there. The person that owned the Demary Placer, his former property near Leadville showed us the road that Hiram helped to get built and the log cabin where he spent his first winter.

France: Two trips visiting one of the places where my grandfather Jack was stationed during WWI.

I learned a lot about my mother's father by reading and transcribing the letters that he sent home from France during World War One. I thought that by visiting some of the locations that he wrote about I could feel a little closer to him. In 2011 I planed a trip to Is-sur-Tille in the Burgundy region of France where he spent six weeks and wrote twelve of his letters.

While searching the Internet I was delighted to find information about Camp Williams on the websites of the Société d'Histoire Tille-Ignon and the town of Is-sur-Tille. When I first sent the historical society the descriptive portions of the letters I was hoping that they could tell me where to find some of the locations that my grandfather had described. What I received was much more.

When we arrived, only a few minutes late, at the home of our contact, Pierre, he was waiting for us out by the road. After driving in we were introduced to: Pierre's wife; the assistant mayor Christian, and his wife, who both taught English at the local schools, and Jean Marc who had a WWII American Jeep. A little while later a reporter for the newspaper and her husband, a photographer, arrived and started taking pictures and asking questions.

I rode in the jeep leading a caravan to Maison Perrenet. This was the home of the miller who had allowed soldiers, probably including my grandfather, to live in his home while the new barracks were being built. We met the current owners and had a tour of the home and property including the mill where the Americans were allowed to install a generator to provide electricity to the camp.

Then we drove to the memorial for "Le Camp American" that had been erected in 2008 by the Societe d'Histoire Tille/Ignon and the Rotary Club, on the 90th anniversary of the camp. Our next stop was a stone chimney that was the only physical remainder of what had been a huge rail and logistics base. That evening we attended a reception for the opening of an art display and then we were taken to a restaurant in town for dinner.

The next morning Barb and I walked with Pierre and his dog to the top of LeMont de Marcilly-sur-Tille, a hill where we were able to view the valley and see the extent of the camp. We could see the the mill, the old chimney, and the surrounding hills that grandpa rode to on a bicycle.

While Christian was giving us a tour of the town we were informally introduced to the mayor while walking through the market. Later at the Hotel de Ville (city hall) we were officially introduced and had photos taken with the mayor in his office and in the main hall where an American Flag has been on display since Le Grand Gare (World War One.) They proudly showed us the War Memorial in the town square that listed the town's WWI and WWII casualties. On the back of the memorial were the names of 238 American soldiers that had died at Camp Williams.

My grandfather wrote about wanting to go to a particular castle that had a drawbridge. I did not ever read that he made it. Pierre and his wife took us to see a walled country home surrounded by a moat that had a working drawbridge. Another letter told about a 1000 year old castle that was "mostly a pile of rubble" so they drove us 10 miles to see the site that they were sure he was writing about.

The letter of 4/7/1918 said "This is a dandy place & the little village near us is very quaint – it reminds me of Venice – as there is a river dashing through it & the houses are built right in the water – so that the women do their washing right from their backdoor – quite a stunt – they have a wooden paddle and beat the wadding out of whatever they are washing on a stone slab." We were invited into a bourgeoisie house in town on a canal where the servants used to wash the clothes at their own lavoir, a washing facility, rather than using a communal one.

The next morning we spent time with Pierre and his wife. On the way out of town we stopped to take a photo of the names of the two Perrenet boys that were listed on the war memorial in Marcilly-sur-Tille, the next town over. It turned out that the 8th of May is a French holiday celebrating the end of World War II in Europe. The mayors of both towns were there along with the local band and an honor guard. The mayor of Is-sur-Tille told me in French that he had been looking for me at their ceremony that morning. With Christian translating I explained that the miller had assisted the Americans because his two sons had been killed and he wanted to help end the war.

After the trip I wrote an article that Christian translated and published in two issues of the town's bulletin which are posted on the town's website. Pierre & Christian translated all of the letters that were written in Is-sur-Tille and they were published in the 2011 journal of the SHTI.

In 2012 we decided to return and arranged to arrive on the 7th of May so that we could take part in events. On the morning of 8 Mai we joined everyone in the parking lot of a park near our hotel. After numerous handshakes and "bonjours" a group of veterans, the mayor, an official from Dijon, the pompiers (fireman and emergency workers), the local band, and guests including Barb and I walked down the streets to the War Memorial. During the ceremony I said hello to the mayor's wife and then heard the mayor introducing me. He mentioned my grandfather being stationed there and about me wanting to walk in his footsteps. After the ceremony most of the people went inside for an informal reception with coffee and Kir Pamplemousse (white wine and grapefruit juice). The mayor then told a little about my prior visit and my grandfather's letters. Christian mentioned the online articles and after telling the story about the mayor looking for me last year and how we had decided to return this year, everyone applauded. Pierre, the mayor, and their wives then joined us at Christian's home for a wonderful lunch. We spent several days exploring the town and I was even invited to attend a city council meeting.

Thatched Roofed Building

The old chimney was the only site that I visited and was sure that it was the same place that my grandfather described. It was part of a building that he wrote about in several letters.

13 April 1918 - "There was a company of English stationed here once & the non-commissioned got busy & built a house, built the furniture, fireplace & everything else – it is very attractive – has a thatched roof & the sides are made of home made adobe (straw & clay) the interior is rustic – whole trees for beams & big rocks for fire place. The chair seats & backs are woven of reeds & branches."

In 2012 I returned to the chimney. The area was not as overgrown as before. I was able to locate some moss covered round rocks in the area where I believe that the second chimney would have been. While I was looking around a gentleman stopped and left his car on the highway to come over and tell us that the former hospital and reservoir had been on the hill above us. It turned out that he was one of the people responsible for updating the names of the Americans on the war memorial after they could no longer be read.

My wife and I had a wonderful and unique experience thanks in great part to our hosts, the mayor, and the families that opened up their homes and gave us a glimpse of what life was like then, and now.

Being able to meet with and talk with local people, or at least try to, is what makes any trip special. I was able to not only connect a little bit with my grandfather, but with the town and the surrounding area that he loved, and a few of the people living there. While my grandfather was never able to return to France as he had wished, I have been there four times and plan on returning.

Finding Alvar, A Not So Great Dane!

This condensed 2006 case study might provide a little hope for those researching a "missing person." It describes the long quest to find my grandfather, Alvar Bockman, who left the family when my father was only five years old. Hopefully it will also encourage people to save information and write about those individuals that they would just as soon forget, because future generations will be curious and your efforts could save them years of research.

When the Social Security Death Index first became available around 1997, I searched for all people named Alvar that were born in 1890 and 1891. It listed four individuals but none of the names were close to Bockman. At that time there was no easy way to research them, so I put a copy of the information in my brickwall lecture folder.

For years I wished that my grandmother had left some information about Alvar. Well it turned out that she did. In 2002, while visiting the NARA facility in Chicago I requested her naturalization records and her Declaration of Intent gave Alvar's birthday as 25 January 1891. That fits within the 12/21/1890 to 2/25/1891 range determined on page 33. I updated my Ancestor Chart, the computerized Family Group Sheet, and timelines but I did not go back and review the entire file.

> **Review Old Records!** {Do as I say, not as I do!} After obtaining new information, update family information and timelines, and then review the file and make any new conclusions.

In early 2005, while preparing for a lecture I came across the list of Alvars. This time I noticed that an Alvar Anderson who had died in Michigan in 1965 had the same date of birth as my Alvar.

I immediately checked the 1930 Census Index and found two Alvar Andersons living in Michigan. The closest one by age showed that he was born in 1893 in Pennsylvania. Even though I was extremely disappointed I still clicked on "View Record." The image showed that this Alvar had been born in Panama (not Pennsylvania) to a Swedish father and a German mother. His age was given as 37 instead of 39. It showed that he had a wife and 1 8/12 year old son and that they were living in his father-in-law's household and that his occupation was a painter.

I quickly checked the 1920 and 1910 Census indexes to see if this Alvar Anderson was listed. He was not. I had previously checked to see if Alvar Bockman was listed in 1930 and he was not. Alvar was not a very common name as there were only 157 people with that name in the 1920 Census. There were only 2,629 people born on 25 January 1891 in the SSDI. Alvar Bockman's occupation on the birth certificate of his fourth child was also a painter. Alvar Anderson, as they currently say on newscasts, was now "a person of interest."

A Person of Interest

It looked like Alvar Anderson's SS card had been issued in Detroit, Michigan so I checked the Detroit index of naturalizations at the National Archives, but he was not listed.

I did find Alvar Anderson listed in the 1931 Polk's city directory for Jackson, MI still living at the residence of his father-in-law.

In March of 2005 I went to Jackson, Michigan to see what I could find. I obtained the death certificates for his wife and son but there was nothing for Alvar. They would not show me the son's birth certificate due to a one hundred-year privacy law. The wife's obituary stated that she was survived by a son and daughter. A visit to the cemetery showed that Alvar was not buried with the rest of the family. City directories for 1938, 1947, 1949, 1959, 1962, and 1964 showed his wife listed as the widow of Alvar. Was Alvar really dead or was "widow" the politically correct entry for an abandoned wife?

A call to the surviving son was a very interesting experience. How do you tactfully approach this subject? Things went a little easier when I asked if he was the son of Alvar Anderson and he said "No." I was a bit surprised but I verified that his mother was the person listed as Alvar's wife. I think I then asked, "Well, who was your father?" After he answered Fred I knew that I was not going to destroy Ozzie and Harriet's household. We ended up having a very nice conversation. I was told that his mother had left home and returned with Alvar and a young son who had Down's syndrome. He said that Alvar had left after several years and was never heard from again. I asked about any pictures and he had seen one but did not know of any copies. He said that Alvar was good looking By now I was beginning to doubt the old family stories about Alvar and Central America.

Alvar Anderson's SSDI death date was Jan 1965. During a visit to a local Social Security office they provided me with a document, A55 which had a list of his yearly earnings since 1951. It showed very little earnings for 1965. I requested his SS-5 (Application for Account Number) in March of 2005 and then waited, and waited. I e-mailed a follow-up inquiry, talked to one representative on the phone and another in person and still received nothing. I finally mailed another inquiry letter to the supervisor in Washington, DC and then I waited some more.

Keep Looking for New Online Resources - Procrastination finally paid off. In November of 2005 the WWI Draft Records went online at Ancestry.com. My "Exact Name" search for Alvar Bockman that usually brought up only the 1920 Census now had two other entries.

First was his WWI Draft Registration Card 1917-1918 that I hadn't been able to previously locate. It gave his name as Alvar Reginaldt Sedoff Bockman, birth date as Jan. 25, 1891, and birthplace as Lucastes, Nicaragua. The record listed him as single. It had been filled out after obtaining their marriage license but before they were married. It showed that he was a waiter at a restaurant kitty-corner to Marshal Fields in Chicago where my grandmother worked. It also included his signature.

The second entry was a Boston Passenger Lists 1820-1943 record. I figured that this would just be a page that listed someone with a first name of Alvar and someone else with the name of Bockman, but BINGO! There was a two-year-old Alvar on the ship Nyassa arriving from Pearl Lagoon, Nicaragua on September 1st 1893 traveling with a 36-year-old planter named Theo Bockman and a Mrs. A. Bockman. Their nationality was Dane and their final destination was Denmark. Here was Alvar traveling with his parents! A closer look at the passenger list showed that the only full names shown were Alvar and a young girl named Olga. The rest were all abbreviations or initials. It does not hurt to have a little luck while doing research. Later, a review of my Nicaragua History timeline showed that there was a revolt in 1893 that ended the conservative government. That was probably the reason that Theodore was taking his family back home to Denmark.

I immediately searched Ancestry for Theo and Theodore Bockman and found a New Orleans marriage to an Alva Neuhaus on 5 May 1890. I called and found out that the Louisiana marriage records listed the names of the parents so I immediately requested a copy. Theo & Alva's marriage record arrived quickly and it did list their parent's names. I finally had paternal grandparents and great-grandparents. My Dad's family twig had actually become a small tree and I finally had all of the names for my 5-generation ancestor chart.

I found an April 24th 1890 New Orleans arrival record for Theo Bockman. This was 10 days before his marriage. The newspaper told about the voyage and which hotel he checked into that night.

Did Alvar Bockman become Alvar Anderson?

In the mail on the last day of 2005 was an envelope from the Social Security Administration. Alvar Anderson's SS-5 had finally arrived. It provided the following information:

Name: Alvar Reginald Anderson, His address and employer were both in Detroit, MI
Date of Birth: 25th January 1898 with a handwritten change to 1894 (1891 in the SSDI)
Place of Birth: Bluefields, Central America   Father: Stephen Anderson
Mother: Anna Neuhaus. Dated and signed on January 18, 1937

Did Alvar Bockman become Alvar Anderson? I believe yes. They both have a first name of Alvar, they were both born on January 25, 1891 in Nicaragua, both of their occupations included being a painter, and both of their mother's maiden names were Neuhaus. Their middle names of Reginalt and Reginald and birthplaces are very close. Their signatures, which were twenty years apart, are very similar. All of these similarities along with the fact that they both left young families and that they cannot both be found at the same time makes it appear that they are in fact the same individual.

Where's Alvar

Thanks to a revolution that caused a family to leave Nicaragua and stop in Boston on their way back to Denmark, someone writing Alvar's full name, two Danish citizens, one living in Nicaragua, getting married in New Orleans, Ancestry posting several records and indexes, along with some good old-fashioned research, and a little luck, I finally had great-and great-great-grandparents.

I had always said that I didn't really care that much about Alvar and that all I really wanted was to find his parents so that I could continue with my research. Well, I lied. Being the natural born problem solver that I am, I want to fill in all of the blanks.

Back in 2006 I had a lot of questions. Did he really die in Jan. 1965? If so, Where? I did not find an obituary in the January 1st - 26[th,] 1965 issues of the Detroit News. Where and when did he die? Where is he buried? What was he doing between 1937 and 1965? Was the Anna Neuhaus listed as his mother on the SS5 the lady that left Denmark for New Orleans? Was she his aunt? Did Alva remarry a Stephen Anderson or was this just a fictitious name? The 1935, 1938, 1939, 1958 and 1964 Detroit City directories showed an Alvar Anderson with a wife. Was this my Alvar with another family? Does anyone have a picture of him?

Since 2006 I obtained Alvar Anderson's MI death certificate. The informant, his employer, gave the correct birth date and Bluefields, Nicaragua as the birthplace. It said that Alvar was "never married" so that proved to me that Alvar was very good at keeping a secret. It also gave the name of the cemetery in Detroit where I found out that he was buried in a "State" grave with a marker "W235."

I met the son of Alvar's Michigan wife and we had a very nice visit. He showed me pictures of his mother. He was interested in finding out what happened to Alvar.

An 1894 New York Times article datelined Mobile, Alabama told of the arrival of a Theodor Bockman, a well-to-do planter from Rama (a town inland from Bluefields). An 1895 Danish departure record for Aloa (Alva) also showed her heading to Mobile Alabama. The 1895 and 1896 Mobile city directories showed Theodore running Bayside Nursery. Checking the court records for the sale of the property I noticed "EST" (The Estate of) on a number of records indicating that Theodore had died. His probate records showed that he had died on 18 July 1896 in Bocas Del Toro, Columbia (now Panama) and that he had been buried there at an unknown location. The probate records proved that Theodor and Alva were Alvar's parents and they also showed that in 1898 Alva and Alvar were living in Copenhagen.

Now I have to find out: What Alvar was doing between 1898 and 1917, What happened to Alva? Did she marry Stephen Anderson? I also have more research to do on the great-great grandparents.

I hope that you are as fortunate in your search for your "missing person." Good Luck

Our Family

This Book was compiled for the

_____

Family

by: _____

_____

_____

_____

Filling in Your Forms

The following pages contain:

Three (3) Family Group Sheets, one (1) Ancestor chart, two (2) Timeslines, and a Notes page.

If additional forms are needed these may be photocopied or you can download and print them from the website www.JeffBockman.com/forms.

Family Group Sheets

Create a Family Group Sheet for:

1. The family that you and your partner had
2. You as a child; list your Father, Mother, and siblings
3. You partner as a child; list their Father, Mother, and siblings

You could also create Family Group Sheets (make additional copies) for

4. Your Mother as a Child *   This will list your grandparents, aunts and uncles
5. Your Father as a Child *   This will list your grandparents, aunts and uncles
6. Your Partners' Mother as a Child *
7. Your Partners' Father as a Child *

   *Create one even if you do not know the names of the parents but you know the names of some of the sisters and brothers.

Ancestor Charts

o Leave #1 blank, or enter the information if you have an only child
o You and your spouse are #2 and #3.
o Your parents and in-laws are #4 - #7, etc.
o Make copies and enter the information in #1 for each child

Timelines

Fill out one Timeline for you. The other could be for your spouse or used as a continuation.

Notes

Use this page to tell where any additional forms, photographs and family stories are stored.

Additional Forms & Information

Go to www.JeffBockman.com/agift for:

➢ Forms to download:
  ▪ Home Sources List
  ▪ Ancestor Chart
  ▪ Family Group Sheet
  ▪ Timeline
➢ Links to preservation and other product information

Family Group Sheet

Father's Full Name

Chart No.

	Day Month Year	City, Town or Place	County or Province, etc.	State or Country	Add. Info. on Husband
Birth					
Chr'nd					
Marr.					
Death					
Burial					

Places of Residence

Occupation	Church Affiliation	Military Rec.

Other wives, if any. No. (1) (2) etc.
Make separate sheet for each marr.

His Father	Mother's Maiden Name

Mother's Full Maiden Name

	Day Month Year	City, Town or Place	County or Province, etc.	State or Country	Add. Info. on Wife
Birth					
Chr'nd					
Death					
Burial					

Places of Residence

Occupation	Church Affiliation	Military Rec.

Other husbands, if any. No. (1) (2) etc.
Make separate sheet for each marr.

Her Father	Mother's Maiden Name

Sex	Children's Names in Full (Arranged in order of birth)	Children's Data	Day Month Year	City, Town or Place	County or Province, etc.	State or Country	Add. Info on Children
	1	Birth					
		Marr.					
	Full Name of Spouse	Death					
		Burial					
	2	Birth					
		Marr.					
	Full Name of Spouse	Death					
		Burial					
	3	Birth					
		Marr.					
	Full Name of Spouse	Death					
		Burial					
	4	Birth					
		Marr.					
	Full Name of Spouse	Death					
		Burial					
	5	Birth					
		Marr.					
	Full Name of Spouse	Death					
		Burial					
	6	Birth					
		Marr.					
	Full Name of Spouse	Death					
		Burial					
	7	Birth					
		Marr.					
	Full Name of Spouse	Death					
		Burial					
	8	Birth					
		Marr.					
	Full Name of Spouse	Death					
		Burial					

Compiler	Notes:
Address	
City, State, Zip	

"A Gift That Money Can't Buy"

Additional Children and Sources:

Father's name: _____   **Mother's name:** _____

Sex	Children's Names in Full (Arranged in order of birth)	Children's Data	Day	Month	Year	City, Town or Place	County or Province, etc.	State or Country	Add. Info on Children
	9	Birth							
		Marr.							
	Full Name of Spouse	Death							
		Burial							
	10	Birth							
		Marr.							
	Full Name of Spouse	Death							
		Burial							
	11	Birth							
		Marr.							
	Full Name of Spouse	Death							
		Burial							
	12	Birth							
		Marr.							
	Full Name of Spouse	Death							
		Burial							
	13	Birth							
		Marr.							
	Full Name of Spouse	Death							
		Burial							
	14	Birth							
		Marr.							
	Full Name of Spouse	Death							
		Burial							
	15	Birth							
		Marr.							
	Full Name of Spouse	Death							
		Burial							

Sources for Father:

Sources for Mother:

Sources for Children:

Additional Information:

Family Group Sheet

Father's Full Name

Chart No.

	Day Month Year	City, Town or Place	County or Province, etc.	State or Country	Add. Info. on Husband
Birth					
Chr'nd					
Marr.					
Death					
Burial					

Places of Residence

Occupation   Church Affiliation   Military Rec.

Other wives, if any. No. (1) (2) etc.
Make separate sheet for each marr.

His Father   Mother's Maiden Name

Mother's Full Maiden Name

	Day Month Year	City, Town or Place	County or Province, etc.	State or Country	Add. Info. on Wife
Birth					
Chr'nd					
Death					
Burial					

Places of Residence

Occupation   Church Affiliation   Military Rec.

Other husbands, if any. No. (1) (2) etc.
Make separate sheet for each marr.

Her Father   Mother's Maiden Name

Sex	Children's Names in Full (Arranged in order of birth)	Children's Data	Day Month Year	City, Town or Place	County or Province, etc.	State or Country	Add. Info on Children
1		Birth					
		Marr.					
	Full Name of Spouse	Death					
		Burial					
2		Birth					
		Marr.					
	Full Name of Spouse	Death					
		Burial					
3		Birth					
		Marr.					
	Full Name of Spouse	Death					
		Burial					
4		Birth					
		Marr.					
	Full Name of Spouse	Death					
		Burial					
5		Birth					
		Marr.					
	Full Name of Spouse	Death					
		Burial					
6		Birth					
		Marr.					
	Full Name of Spouse	Death					
		Burial					
7		Birth					
		Marr.					
	Full Name of Spouse	Death					
		Burial					
8		Birth					
		Marr.					
	Full Name of Spouse	Death					
		Burial					

Compiler   Notes:

Address

City, State, Zip

"A Gift That Money Can't Buy"

Additional Children and Sources:

Father's name: _____   **Mother's name:** _____

Sex	Children's Names in Full (Arranged in order of birth)	Children's Data	Day Month Year	City, Town or Place	County or Province, etc.	State or Country	Add. Info on Children
	9	Birth					
		Marr.					
	Full Name of Spouse	Death					
		Burial					
	10	Birth					
		Marr.					
	Full Name of Spouse	Death					
		Burial					
	11	Birth					
		Marr.					
	Full Name of Spouse	Death					
		Burial					
	12	Birth					
		Marr.					
	Full Name of Spouse	Death					
		Burial					
	13	Birth					
		Marr.					
	Full Name of Spouse	Death					
		Burial					
	14	Birth					
		Marr.					
	Full Name of Spouse	Death					
		Burial					
	15	Birth					
		Marr.					
	Full Name of Spouse	Death					
		Burial					

Sources for Father:

Sources for Mother:

Sources for Children:

Additional Information:

Family Group Sheet

Father's Full Name

Chart No.

	Day Month Year	City, Town or Place	County or Province, etc.	State or Country	Add. Info. on Husband
Birth					
Chr'nd					
Marr.					
Death					
Burial					

Places of Residence

Occupation	Church Affiliation	Military Rec.

Other wives, if any. No. (1) (2) etc.
Make separate sheet for each marr.

His Father	Mother's Maiden Name

Mother's Full Maiden Name

	Day Month Year	City, Town or Place	County or Province, etc.	State or Country	Add. Info. on Wife
Birth					
Chr'nd					
Death					
Burial					

Places of Residence

Occupation	Church Affiliation	Military Rec.

Other husbands, if any. No. (1) (2) etc.
Make separate sheet for each marr.

Her Father	Mother's Maiden Name

Sex	Children's Names in Full (Arranged in order of birth)	Children's Data	Day Month Year	City, Town or Place	County or Province, etc.	State or Country	Add. Info on Children
	1	Birth					
		Marr.					
	Full Name of Spouse	Death					
		Burial					
	2	Birth					
		Marr.					
	Full Name of Spouse	Death					
		Burial					
	3	Birth					
		Marr.					
	Full Name of Spouse	Death					
		Burial					
	4	Birth					
		Marr.					
	Full Name of Spouse	Death					
		Burial					
	5	Birth					
		Marr.					
	Full Name of Spouse	Death					
		Burial					
	6	Birth					
		Marr.					
	Full Name of Spouse	Death					
		Burial					
	7	Birth					
		Marr.					
	Full Name of Spouse	Death					
		Burial					
	8	Birth					
		Marr.					
	Full Name of Spouse	Death					
		Burial					

Compiler	Notes:
Address	
City, State, Zip	

"A Gift That Money Can't Buy"

Additional Children and Sources:

Father's name: _____   **Mother's name:** _____

Sex	Children's Names in Full (Arranged in order of birth)	Children's Data	Day Month Year	City, Town or Place	County or Province, etc.	State or Country	Add. info on Children
	9	Birth					
		Marr.					
	Full Name of Spouse	Death					
		Burial					
	10	Birth					
		Marr.					
	Full Name of Spouse	Death					
		Burial					
	11	Birth					
		Marr.					
	Full Name of Spouse	Death					
		Burial					
	12	Birth					
		Marr.					
	Full Name of Spouse	Death					
		Burial					
	13	Birth					
		Marr.					
	Full Name of Spouse	Death					
		Burial					
	14	Birth					
		Marr.					
	Full Name of Spouse	Death					
		Burial					
	15	Birth					
		Marr.					
	Full Name of Spouse	Death					
		Burial					

Sources for Father:

Sources for Mother:

Sources for Children:

Additional Information:

Ancestor Chart

Name of Compiler_____

Address_____

City, State_____

Date_____

Person No. 1 on this chart is the same
person as No._____on chart No._____.

Chart No._____

b. Date of Birth
p.b. Place of Birth
m. Date of Marriage
d. Date of Death
p.d. Place of Death

16
b.
m.
d.
(Father of No. 8,
Cont. on chart No._____)

17
b.
d.
(Mother of No. 8,
Cont. on chart No._____)

8
b.
p.b.
m.
d.
p.d
(Father of No. 4)

18
b.
m.
d.
(Father of No. 9,
Cont. on chart No._____)

19
b.
d.
(Mother of No. 9,
Cont. on chart No._____)

9
b.
p.b.
d.
p.d
(Mother of No. 4)

4
b.
p.b.
m.
d.
p.d
(Father of No. 2)

2
b.
p.b.
m.
d.
p.d
(Father of No. 1)

20
b.
m.
d.
(Father of No. 10,
Cont. on chart No._____)

21
b.
d.
(Mother of No. 10,
Cont. on chart No._____)

10
b.
p.b.
m.
d.
p.d
(Father of No. 5)

22
b.
m.
d.
(Father of No. 11,
Cont. on chart No._____)

23
b.
d.
(Mother of No. 11,
Cont. on chart No._____)

5
b.
p.b.
d.
p.d.
(Mother of No. 2)

11
b.
p.b.
d.
p.d
(Mother of No. 5)

1_____
b.
p.b.
m.
d.
p.d.

24
b.
m.
d.
(Father of No. 12,
Cont. on chart No._____)

25
b.
d.
(Mother of No. 12,
Cont. on chart No._____)

12
b.
p.b.
m.
d.
p.d
(Father of No. 6)

26
b.
m.
d.
(Father of No. 13,
Cont. on chart No._____)

27
b.
d.
(Mother of No. 13,
Cont. on chart No._____)

6
b.
p.b.
m.
d.
p.d
(Father of No. 3)

13
b.
p.b.
d.
p.d.
(Mother of No. 6)

3
b.
p.b.
d.
p.d.
(Mother of No. 1)

28
b.
m.
d.
(Father of No. 14,
Cont. on chart No._____)

29
b.
d.
(Mother of No. 14,
Cont. on chart No._____)

14
b.
p.b.
m.
d.
p.d
(Father of No. 7)

30
b.
m.
d.
(Father of No. 15,
Cont. on chart No._____)

31
b.
d.
(Mother of No. 15,
Cont. on chart No._____)

7
b.
p.b.
d.
p.d.
(Mother of No. 3)

15
b.
p.b.
d.
p.d.
(Mother of No. 7)

_____
(Spouse of No. 1)
b.
p.b.
d.
p.d.

"A Gift That Money Can't Buy"

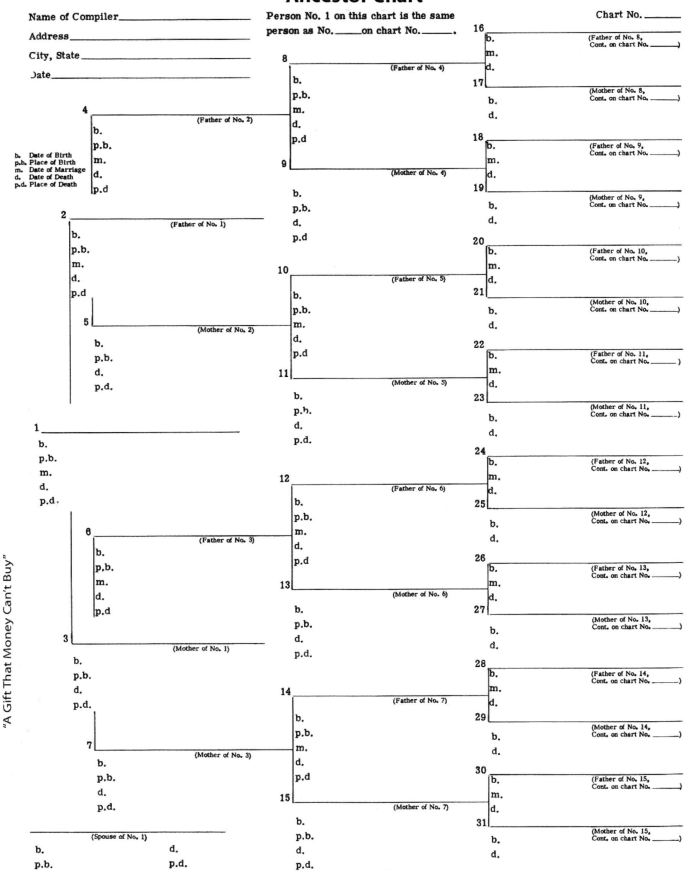

Timeline

Full Name:		
Date	**Event**	**Comments**
	Birth	

Compiled by:

Timeline

Full Name:		
Date	**Event**	**Comments**

Compiled by:

Notes